Competition Law in Zambia

Competition Law in Zambia

Chanda Chungu

This book was originally published as a monograph in the International Encyclopaedia of Laws/Competition Law.

Founding Editor: Roger Blanpain
General Editor: Frank Hendrickx
Volume Editors: Francesco Denozza & Alberto Toffoletto

Wolters Kluwer

Published by:
Kluwer Law International B.V.
PO Box 316
2400 AH Alphen aan den Rijn
The Netherlands
E-mail: international-sales@wolterskluwer.com
Website: www.wolterskluwer.com/en/solutions/kluwerlawinternational

Sold and distributed by:
Wolters Kluwer Legal & Regulatory U.S.
7201 McKinney Circle
Frederick, MD 21704
United States of America
E-mail: customer.service@wolterskluwer.com

ISBN 978-94-035-4215-7

e-Book: ISBN 978-94-035-4220-1
web-PDF: ISBN 978-94-035-4221-8

The Author

Mr Chanda Chungu is a Lecturer at the University of Zambia (UNZA). He obtained both his Bachelor of Laws (LLB) and Master's of Laws (LLM) in Commercial and Labour Law from the University of Cape Town. His research interests are in labour law, industrial relations, administrative and constitutional law. He was previously a Teaching Assistant and Junior Lecturer at the University of Cape Town as well as a researcher for the International Labour Organisation and the World Bank Africa Mining Project. He also served for two years on the University of Cape Town Council and Senate. He is currently completing his Doctor of Philosophy (PhD) degree at the University of Cape Town.

The Author

Table of Contents

List of Abbreviations

BOZ	Bank of Zambia
CCPC	Competition and Consumer Protection Commission
DMMU	DevDisaster Management and Mitigation Unitelopment
GDP	Gross Domestic Product
LAZ	Law Association of Zambia
NAPSA	National Pension Scheme Authority
PACRA	Patents and Companies Registry Agency
PIA	Pensions and Insurance Authority
ZMW	Zambian Kwacha
ZNPF	Zambia National Provident Fund
ZRA	Zambia Revenue Authority

List of Abbreviations

Preface and Acknowledgements

This publication seeks to provide an extensive overview of Zambia's competition law. The publication is the first publication of its kind to consider Zambia's Competition and Consumer Protection Act and analyse critical aspects of the legislation in relation to restrictive agreements, abuse of dominance, legal exceptions, merger control and the powers of the Competition and Consumer Protection Commission and Tribunal.

The author is grateful to the IEL team for the opportunity and the Zambian Supreme Court library for access to numerous case law that was referred to in this publication.

The author is grateful to his parents, the late Mr Chisanga Chungu and Mrs Manyando Siachinji Chungu and his sister Moono Chungu for their support rendered throughout and encouragement during the best and worst of times.

General Introduction

§1. General Background of the Country

1. Zambia is a Sub-Saharan country and is located in southern Africa, east of Angola, between the latitudes 8S and 18S and longitudes 20E and 35E. It is land-locked, sharing its borders with eight neighbours: Angola, Botswana, Namibia, Zimbabwe, Mozambique, Malawi, Tanzania and the Democratic Republic of Congo. Its total landmass is 752, 614 square kilometres and the capital city Lusaka is located in the south-central part of the country.

2. The country is divided into ten provinces namely Southern, Western, North-Western, Copperbelt, Central, Luapula, Northern, Muchinga, Eastern and Lusaka. The provinces are further subdivided into a total of 117 districts.

3. Zambia has been a parliamentary democracy since 1991, with a multiparty political system, and is generally regarded as a peaceful nation. Prior to this, in 1972, Zambia entered into nearly two decades of one-party state rule that led to the suppression of political opposition.

4. Presidential and parliamentary elections are held every five years.

5. The term of the President runs currently with the term of office of members of the National Assembly, the legislative arm of government. Zambia is divided into constituencies and wards for purposes of elections to the National Assembly and councils, respectively.

6. Elections to the National Assembly shall be conducted under a first-past-the-post electoral system. The National Assembly consists of 156 members directly elected on the basis of a simple majority vote under the first-past-the-post system; not more than eight nominated members; the Vice President; the Speaker; and the First and Second Deputy Speakers.

7. Parliament shall enact legislation through Bills passed by the National Assembly and assented to by the President.

8. The National Assembly shall oversee the performance of executive functions by:

- ensuring equity in the distribution of national resources amongst the people of Zambia;
- appropriating funds for expenditure by State organs, State institutions, provincial administration, local authorities and other bodies;
- scrutinising public expenditure, including defence, constitutional and special expenditure;
- approving public debt before it is contracted; and
- approving international agreements and treaties before these are acceded to or ratified.

9. The judiciary consists of a Constitutional Court which hears cases relating to constitutional issues, the Supreme court which is the highest court for all non-constitutional matters and the Court of Appeal and the High Court – with judges appointed by the President and ratified by the National Assembly – and provincial high courts spread across its nine provinces. The country also has an Industrial Relations Division of the High Court. The judicial system is further complemented by a number of subordinate courts namely magistrate and local courts.

10. The population is concentrated mainly around the capital Lusaka in the south and in the Copperbelt to the northwest. Zambia's population is estimated at 16,405,229 (as at November 2018) is mostly young, but is growing steadily and is projected to reach about and 21.5 million by 2025. However, this steady increase has been affected by the recent developments in urban growth and the spread of HIV/AIDS.

11. Zambia is officially a Christian country as Christianity enshrined in the Constitution as the state religion.[1] The Constitution also says that Zambian society is tolerant of other religions, and the right to express these religions is protected in Article 19.

12. According to Article 8 of the Constitution, the national values and principles are:

(1) morality and ethics;
(2) patriotism and national unity;
(3) democracy and constitutionalism;
(4) human dignity, equity, social justice, equality and non-discrimination;
(5) good governance and integrity; and
(6) sustainable development.

13. The national values and principles shall apply to the interpretation of this Constitution; enactment and interpretation of the law; and development and implementation of State policy.

1. Preamble to the Constitution of Zambia.

14. The President shall, once in every year, report to the National Assembly the progress made in the application of the values and principles specified under this Part.

§2. Economic System

15. Around 60% of Zambia's population are living below the poverty line and 43% of these are classified as extremely poor. In 2010, the Gross Domestic Product (GDP) was 7.6%, the highest level recorded since 1972. As of 2018, the GDP was 4.2%

16. Zambia's economic performance has continued to improve and the continued growth has been driven by increased output in Construction, Mining and Agriculture sector. In 2012, the average GDP growth rate was 7.3%.

17. In 2013, real GDP growth continued to be positive with preliminary figures indicating a growth rate of 6.4%. This drop from the 7.3% recorded in 2012 is mainly attributed to a decline in the agriculture output as well as a slowdown in the manufacturing and construction sectors.

18. Zambia's population has been increasing at an annual average rate of 2.8%. The population was estimated at 7,383,097 in 1990, and increased to 9,885,591 in 2000 and to 13,092,666 in 2010. This represented a percentage increase of 33.9% in the 1990-2000 intercensal period. Between 2000 and 2010, the percentage increase was 32.4%.

19. The 2017 projected population was estimated at 16,405,229. Zambia has more people living in rural areas than urban areas. Rural population accounted for 60.6% in 1990, 65.3% in 2000 and 60.5% in 2010. Copperbelt and Lusaka Provinces are the highly populated provinces. In 2000, Copperbelt Province had 16.0% of the total population while Lusaka Province had 14.1%. In 2010, Lusaka Province had 16.7% of the total population while Copperbelt Province had 15.1%. Muchinga Province accounting for the lowest at 5.4%.

20. Furthermore, Zambia has a young population. About 46.6% of the total population is below 15 years of age inclusive while persons aged 65 years or older account for 2.6% of the total population.

21. Zambia's economy is driven by the Mining, Agriculture, Construction, Transport and Communication industries. However, recent economic data shows that the largest percentage share of the GDP is the Wholesale and Retail trade industry. Between 2015 and 2017, Zambia's real GDP was between ZMW 125,003.5 million and ZMW 134, 998.0 million. The Wholesale and Retail trade sector accounting for 22% in 2015, 22.1% in 2016 and 22.9% in 2017.

22. The Mining and Agriculture industries accounted for 10.2% and 7.3% of the GDP, respectively. In 2010, the annual real GDP growth was 7.6%, the highest level ever recorded since 1972, while in 2017, the annual real GDP growth was 4.1%. Zambia's annual inflation rate between 2015 and 2017 trended from 10.0% in 2015 to 18.2% in 2016 and to 6.5% in 2017.

23. Trends in the labour force since 1986-2014, Zambia's labour force has been increasing. In 2005, the population in the labour force was estimated at 4,918,788, giving rise to a labour force participation rate of 80.0%. The Labour Force grew to 5,003,871 in 2008 and 5,966,199 in 2012 giving participation rates of 74.5% and 75.9%, respectively. In 2014, the population in the labour force was 6,329,076 which gave rise to the participation rate of 77.7%.

24. The employed population has slowly been moving from agriculture industries to non-agriculture industry between 2005 to 2014. In 2005, agriculture industry accounted for 73.0% of the employed population rate in 2012, the industry accounted for 52.2%. In 2014, agriculture industry accounted for 48.9%. The formal sector accounted 16.4% of the employed population while the informal sector accounted for 88.6%.

25. Paid employees accounted for 26.1% of the employed population while own account workers (self-employed and employers) accounted for 46.3%.

26. The 2006 and 2010 Living Conditions Monitoring Surveys (LCMSs) results show that poverty levels have remained high at 62.8% in 2006 and 60.5% in 2010. Extreme poverty was recorded at 42.7% in 2006 and 42.3% in 2010. In 2015, extreme poverty was recorded at 54.4%.

27. The level of poverty in the rural areas was higher than in urban areas. Rural poverty was estimated at 76.6% compared to the urban poverty at 23.4%.

28. The working-age population was estimated at 9,483,400 of which 53.7% were in the rural areas and 46.3% were in the urban areas.

29. At national level, females account for a higher percentage of the working-age population at 52.3% compared to males at 47.7%. In rural and urban areas, females had a higher percentage of the working-age population than males at 52.2% and 52.4%, respectively.

30. Lusaka provincial had the highest percentage share of the working-age population with 20.4% while North-western had the least share at 5.0%.

31. At national level, the percentage of males in the labour force was higher than that of females at 61.3% and 38.7%, respectively. The same pattern of having more males than females was also observed in both rural and urban areas.

32. Labour force participation rate measures the proportion of the labour force in relation to the working-age population. It is a ratio of the labour force to the working-age population expressed as a percentage. Low activity rate implies that a large proportion of persons are not participating in the labour market.

33. In 2018, the overall labour force participation rate was 35.1%. Males had a higher participation rate at 45.1 compared to females at 26.0%. The urban participation was higher than that of the rural at 47.0% and 24.8%, respectively. The pattern of having higher participation rate for males than females was observed in both rural and urban areas.

34. In 2018, the total number of the unemployed persons was estimated at 380,176. Of the total unemployed persons, 35.2% were in rural areas and 64.8% in urban areas.

35. At national level, the percentage distribution of the unemployed persons by sex shows that 56.4% were males while 43.6% were females. In rural areas, 62.1% were males while 37.9% were females. In urban areas, 53.2% were males while 46.8% were females.

36. In 2018, the total number of the unemployed persons was estimated at 380,176. Of the total unemployed persons, 35.2% were in rural areas and 64.8% in urban areas. Table 11.2 shows the number and percentage distribution of unemployed persons by province and sex. In all the provinces, there were more male unemployed persons than females except in Central and Western provinces which had more females than males at 53.3% and 70.3%, respectively.

37. The preamble of the Zambian Constitution not only recognises the right to work but also gives protection against unemployment. It states

> [r]ecognizing the right to work, to free choice of employment, to just and favourable conditions of work and to protection against unemployment.

It also pledges 'to all citizens the right to equal access to social, economic and cultural services and facilities provided by the State or by public authorities'.

38. In recent years, the performance of the Zambian economy has improved with respect to major macroeconomic indicators, although in recent years the economy experienced a slight slowdown as a result of the fall in copper prices and rising government debt. Whereas, in 1994, mining production represented around 17% of real GDP, it accounted for a little more than 12% of GDP in 2018 due to not only declining prices, but also efforts to increase diversification of the economy. Annual average inflation rates shifted from 6.98% in 2013 to 7.78% in 2014.

39. Additionally, Zambia's export trade has generally increased in the various categories of export products – including Traditional Exports (mainly metals – copper and cobalt) and Non-Traditional Exports (NTEs). As of May 2018, Traditional

Exports accounted for an average contribution of about 78.9% whereas NTEs had a share of about 21.1% of the total export earnings.

40. The growth in the Agriculture, Forestry and Fishing sector increased by 33.6% in 2017-2018 and contributed just under 1% to the GDP growth of the country. Notwithstanding the negative growth in the agriculture sub-sector, the country is still able to maintain food security and sufficient stocks to meet industrial requirements. Total copper production currently stands at 79,516.6 metric tonnes, as of 2018. The growth was attributed to a 12.3% increase in copper output to 783,468 Mt from 697,918 Mt in 2012 by large mines. Due to these various developments, international rating agencies recently revised Zambia's outlook from stable to positive, and affirmed the country's ceiling at B+.

41. The scourge of HIV/AIDS has had a devastating effect on the economy. With a prevalence rate of 11.5% in 2018, a 3% drop since 2012 it affects a large segment of the population. Consequently, child-headed households and child labour, particularly in the informal economy, have become widespread problems.

42. Zambia is home to approximately seventy ethnic groupings with diverse traditions, customs and languages. Linguistically there are some eighty different identified languages, most of them of the Bantu family. For educational and administrative purposes, seven main languages are recognised: Bemba, Lozi, Lunda, Kaonda, Luvale, Tonga, and Nyanja.

43. Bemba, with its various dialects, is widely spoken in northern Zambia and is the lingua franca in the Copperbelt. The Ila and Tonga tongues predominate in the Southern Province. The Nyanja speaking people are found in the eastern province of Zambia, while the Lunda, Kaonda and Luvale speaking people are found mostly in the North-Western province and the Lozis are the dominant group in the Western province of Zambia. English is, however, the official language.

§3. Legal System

44. The Judicature of Zambia is comprised of:

(a) The Constitutional Court of Zambia;
(b) The Supreme Court of Zambia;
(c) The Court of Appeal;
(d) The High Court of Zambia;
(e) The Subordinate Courts;
(f) The Local Courts; and
(g) Such lower courts as may be prescribed by an Act of Parliament.[2]

2. Article 91 (1) of the Constitution of Zambia Revised Edition 1995. The reader should take note that Zambia has been undergoing a Constitutional review exercise which has culminated into the drafting of a new Constitution which is currently in draft form. The new Constitution is likely to be

45. The High Court as constituted by the Constitution is established as the High Court of Judicature for Zambia by section 3 of the High Court Act.[3] It is a Superior Court of Record that, in addition to any other jurisdiction conferred by the Constitution or any other law, possesses and exercises the entire jurisdiction, powers and authorities vested in the High Court of Justice in England.[4]

46. It has unlimited jurisdiction which includes the judicial hearing and determination of matters in difference, the administration or control of property of persons, the power to appoint or control guardians of infants and their estates, and also keepers of the persons and estates of idiots, lunatics and persons of unsound mind who are unable to govern themselves and their estates.[5]

47. Having unlimited jurisdiction, the High Court can also hear and determine industrial and labour relations cases even though the law has granted jurisdiction in these matters to the Industrial Relations courts.[6] However, the court's unlimited jurisdiction does not extend to offences committed outside the territorial boundaries of Zambia.

48. In probate and matrimonial matters, the jurisdiction of the Court is exercised in substantial conformity with the law and practice for the time being in force in England, subject to the Act and rules of Court made in that behalf.[7]

49. The Court administers law and equity concurrently. Where there is a conflict or variance between the rules of equity and the rules of the common law with reference to the same matter, the rules of equity prevail.[8]

50. Article 130 of the Constitution establishes a Court of Appeal that has jurisdiction to hear appeals from all division of the High Court and other courts, except for matters under the exclusive jurisdiction of the Constitutional Court. The Court of Appeal is a new court established by the Constitution (Amendment) Act.[9]

51. The Constitution of Zambia constitutes the Supreme Court of Zambia as a Court. It has jurisdiction to hear and determine appeals in civil and criminal matters from the Court of Appeal. It also has jurisdiction as conferred on it by other laws.[10]

---

passed in the year 2011. Under the new Constitution the composition of the judiciary will be as follows: the Supreme and Constitutional Court; the Court of Appeal; the High Court; the Industrial Relations Court; subordinate courts; local courts and any other courts established by Acts of Parliament.

3. Chapter 27 of the Laws of Zambia.
4. In the case of *Rahim Obaid v. The People (2) Nadehim Quasmi v. The People* (1977) ZR 119 (HC), it was held that in the absence of any practice and procedure in our laws on the issue, our courts will follow the Practice and Procedure of the High court in England.
5. Section 9(2).
6. As the section dealing with the Industrial Relations Court above, has shown.
7. Section 11(1).
8. Section 13.
9. No. 2 of 2016.
10. Article 125(2)(b) of the Constitution.

52. In civil matters an appeal lies to the Court from any judgment of the Court of Appeal, subject to the following exceptions and restrictions, namely, no appeal lies to the Supreme Court from an order for extension of time for appealing from a judgment; from an order of a Judge giving unconditional leave[11] to defend an action; from a judgment given by the High Court in the exercise of its appellate or revisional jurisdiction without leave of the High Court or when such leave is refused, without leave of a Judge of the Supreme Court; from an order of the High Court or any Judge of the High Court made with the consent of the parties or from an order as to costs only which by law is left to the discretion of the court without leave of the court or of the judge who made the order; or if that has been refused, without leave of a judge of the Court; from an order made in chambers by a Judge of the High Court or from an interlocutory order or interlocutory judgment made or given by a Judge of the High Court, without the leave of the Judge or, if that has been refused, without the leave of a Judge of the Supreme Court except in the following cases:

(i) where the liberty of the subject or the custody of infants is concerned;
(ii) where an injunction or the appointment of a receiver is granted or refused;
(iii) in the case of a decision determining the claim of any creditor or the liability of any contributory or the liability of any director or other officer under the Companies Act;
(iv) in the case of a *decree nisi* in a matrimonial cause or judgment or order in any admiralty action determining liability;
(v) in the case of an order on a special case stated under any law relating to arbitration.

53. An appeal lies to the Supreme Court in any civil proceedings upon application for *habeas Corpus* against an order for the release of the person restrained as well as against the refusal of such an order.[12]

54. On the hearing of an appeal in an employment matter or any matter, the Supreme Court may confirm, vary, amend or set aside the judgment appealed from or give such judgment as the case may require.[13] The Supreme Court is the final court of appeal unless the matter involves a dispute relating to the Constitution.

55. If the Supreme Court thinks it necessary or expedient in the interests of justice, it may order the production of any document, exhibit or other thing connected with the proceedings if that is necessary to determine the appeal; order any witness who would have been a competent and compellable witness at the trial to attend and be examined before the Court, whether he was or was not called at the trial, or order the examination of any such witness to be conducted in a manner provided by the rules of court before any Judge of the Court or before any officer of the Court or other person appointed by the Court for the purpose, and allow the admission of any

11. Permission.
12. Section 24 A.
13. Section 25 (1).

deposition so taken before the Court; receive the evidence, if tendered, of any witness (including any party) who is a competent but not compellable witness, and if a party makes application for the purposes, of the husband or wife of that party in cases where the evidence of the husband or wife could not have been given at the trial except on application to the trial Court; remit the case to the High Court for further hearing, with such instructions as regards the taking of further evidence or otherwise as appear to it necessary.

56. If it appears to the Court that a new trial should be held, the Court has the power to set aside the judgment appealed against and order a new trial to be held. Whenever the Court gives instructions for the taking of further evidence, it is obliged to make such order as will secure an opportunity to the parties to the proceedings to examine every witness whose evidence is taken.[14]

§4. Historical Background of Antitrust Law

57. The economic reforms in Zambia witnessed economic transformation from an overly State-controlled socialist economy to a market economy, resulting in the commercialisation and privatisation of State-owned enterprises. Since the economy was previously characterised by monopoly and other dominant State enterprises, the Government sought to put in place a competition enforcement mechanism that would ensure that the gains of privatisation and the new investment that was coming into the country would not be eroded by the anticompetitive conduct of private monopoly and dominant players in the newly liberalised economy.

58. The Competition and Fair Trading Act, Chapter 417 of the Laws of Zambia, was therefore enacted in 1994 by Parliament. The Zambia Competition Commission (ZCC) however, only became operational in May 1997.

59. The Competition and Fair Trading Act preserved market processes by preventing firms from engaging in activities that undermined rather than enhanced overall economic efficiency. It prevented firms from distorting the competitive process through conduct or agreements designed to exclude actual or potential competitors. The law in that regard essentially addressed the problems of monopoly power in three major settings:

(a) arrangements and agreements among otherwise independent firms;
(b) unilateral conduct of single firms in dominant positions; and
(c) combinations of independent firms.

14. Section 25.

60. Two broad principles underlined the law. The first principle was that any behaviour which had the object, or effect, of substantially lessening competition in a market should be prohibited. The main types of anticompetitive conduct which were prohibited included the following:

(a) anticompetitive agreements and exclusionary provisions, including primary and secondary boycotts, with a per se ban on price-fixing and boycotts;
(b) misuse of substantial market power for the purpose of eliminating or damaging a competitor, preventing entry or deterring or preventing competitive conduct;
(c) exclusive dealing which substantially lessens competition, with third line forcing prohibited per se;
(d) resale price maintenance for goods; and
(e) mergers and acquisitions which substantially lessen competition in a substantial market. The second principle was that certain anticompetitive behaviour should be able to be authorised on the basis and grounds of 'economic efficiency'.

61. The enforcement of the Competition and Fair Trading Act, 1994 by the Commission was however beset by a number of problems and constraints, which included:

(a) interpretation and treatment of 'concerted practice' and vertical restraints;
(b) definition of 'merger' and notification of mergers;
(c) coverage of public interest in the Act;
(d) explicit exclusions; and
(e) timetable for decisions on authorisations.

62. A number of other challenges that faced the Commission in its enforcement of the Competition and Fair Trading Act, 1994 were related to: (a) Limited investigative powers; (b) Limited administrative remedies; (c) Wide institutional mandate; and (d) Absence of a leniency programme.

63. The formulation of Zambia's national competition and consumer policy was completed in 2009, fifteen years after the coming into force of the country's competition law through the Competition and Fair Trading Act 1994. The policy as approved by Cabinet comprehensively covers the main elements of such policies.

64. The implementation framework of the policy covered the following areas:

- Institutional arrangements: the institutions that are important in the implementation of the policy include the Commission, sector regulators and the Judiciary, working in close collaboration with other stakeholders;
- Zambia Competition Commission (ZCC) would be the primary institution mandated to implement the policy, and monitor, control and prohibit acts or behaviour which are likely to adversely affect competition, fair trading and consumer welfare in Zambia. The ZCC is now the Competition and Consumer Protection Commission.

- The Judiciary: the Judiciary through the court system should play an important role in enhancing the enforcement mandate of the competition and consumer authority;
- Sector regulators: sector regulators would play a key role in competition and consumer protection enforcement through institutional linkages and coordination with the relevant authority – the sector regulators and ZCC (now the Competition and Consumer Protection Commission) should enter into Memoranda of Understanding (MoU) to ensure coordinated implementation and enforcement of the legal framework;
- Law enforcement agencies: the various law enforcement agencies should coordinate and cooperate with ZCC (now the Competition and Consumer Protection Commission) in the implementation and enforcement of the competition and consumer legislation;
- Legal and regulatory framework: a comprehensive and complementary legal framework facilitates easy enforcement of competition and consumer provisions of the law – however, the Zambian legal framework is comprehensive but fragmented on consumer provisions, making implementation and enforcement difficult. To ease the operations of the relevant implementing agency, the following legislation plays an important role: (a) the Telecommunications Act which provides regulation of the Information Communication Technology (ICT) sector; (b) the Public Health Act which provides for public health and safety, and; (c) the Food and Drugs Act which provides for standards for food and drugs;
- Resource mobilisation and financing: the principal responsibility of the Central Government in the implementation of the policy would be to mobilise both internal and external sources of finances and provide the relevant agency with necessary financial resources to ensure that the competition and consumer authority successfully implements the proposed Government strategies and activities – a direct appropriation from Parliament would be an ideal process; and
- Monitoring and evaluation: the Ministry of Commerce, Trade and Industry should provide political support and facilitate the monitoring of the implementation process and be responsible for evaluating policy benchmarks herein. In monitoring the implementation of the policy ZCC or a successor institution should take the lead implementation role.

65. The experience gained by the Commission in enforcing the Competition and Fair Trading Act, 1994, the weakness of that legislation and the adoption of the comprehensive national competition and consumer policy, led to the revision of the legislation in order to strengthen the enforcement of the country's competition law. In 2010, the Competition and Fair Trading Act, 1994 was repealed and replaced by the Competition and Consumer Protection Act, 2010 (No. 24 of 2010) which is in force today.

Part I. Structure of Antitrust Law and Its Enforcement

Chapter 1. Sources of Antitrust Law

66. The primary source of antitrust law in Zambia is the Competition and Consumer Protection Act.

§1. National Sources

67. The Competition and Consumer Protection Act No. 24 of 2010 was passed by the National Assembly and subsequently assented to on 14th August 2010.

68. The Act came into operation on 8th October 2010 when a Statutory Instrument was signed by Minister. It seeks to

– to continue the existence of the Zambia Competition Commission and rename it as the Competition and Consumer Protection Commission;
– safeguard and promote competition;
– protect consumers against unfair trade practices;
– provide for the establishment of the Competition and Consumer Protection Tribunal;

§2. International Sources

69. The English Extent of Application Act[15] provides that subject to the provisions of the Constitution of Zambia and any other written law, the common law and doctrines of equity apply. It therefore follows that the principles elucidated in established cases apply in Zambia to the extent that they have not been altered by statute.

70. To this end the case developed and adjudicated by the English court and the European Courts of Justice and General Court will apply in giving interpretation to terms and concepts in Zambian competition law.

15. Chapter 4 of the Laws of Zambia.

§3. Secondary Sources

I. Regulations

71. The Competition and Consumer Protection (General) Regulations 2011, and the Competition and Consumer Protection (Tribunal) Rules 2012 have been issued pursuant to sections 87 and 78 respectively of the Competition and Consumer Protection Act.

II. Guidelines

72. In exercise of its powers under section 84 of the Act, the Competition and Consumer Protection Commission is mandated to make guidelines as are necessary for the carrying out of the provisions of the Competition and Consumer Protection Act.

73. Since 2010, the Commission has released the Commission also issued Administrative and Procedural Guidelines in 2014 (the Administrative Guidelines) and the Leniency Programme has come into effect as well as the Fines Guidelines.

74. The Commission has also released the Competition and Consumer Protection Commission Guidelines for Merger Regulations in 2015 and the Settlement Procedure Guidelines in 2016 and the Guidelines on Abuse of Dominance in 2018.

75. The guidelines are read together with the Competition and Consumer Protection Act in giving meaning to the provisions of the said legislation. The guidelines assist enterprises in getting a sense of the conduct that is permitted and not permitted under Zambian law.

§4. Sources' Relation and Hierarchy

76. The Constitution is the supreme law of Zambia.

77. After that legislation ranks higher than case law in Zambia. Therefore the Competition and Consumer Protection Act ranks higher followed by the guidelines made pursuant to the Act.

78. Zambian case law, which includes decisions of the Competition and Consumer Protection Tribunal follow in terms of hierarchy and thereafter, persuasive case law from the European courts.

§5. Role and Authority of Precedents

79. The case law as developed by the courts of Zambia is another critical aspect of contract law in Zambia. The body of jurisprudence provides precedent on important contract law principles.

Chapter 2. Scope of Application

§1. Territorial Reach

80. The Competition and Consumer Protection Act applies to all economic activity within, or having an effect within, Zambia – Section 3(1). The previous Act did not specify the scope of operation in this manner but just outlined the exemptions.

81. The Act applies to all economic activity within, or having an effect within, Zambia. The meaning of 'having an effect within' may connote that an anticompetitive conduct may be exercised outside Zambia but if it has an effect in Zambia, then the Competition and Consumer Protection Commission can intervene.

82. The concept of public interest has been introduced formally in the new Act, particularly in the examination and determination of mergers. Except for the formulation of two subsections of the relevant provision, the public interest issues are clearly outlined in the Act, and include the promotion of exports and employment, and the protection of micro and small business enterprises. This recognises the fact that competition policy in developing countries should be implemented in coherence with the country's other socio-economic policies for effective economic development.

83. The provisions in the Competition and Consumer Protection Act do not apply to special sectors and statutory monopolies in certain contexts as will be explored below.

84. Further, sections 3(1)(a) to (d) provide that the Competition and Consumer Protection Act do not apply to an agreement or conduct insofar as it relates to intellectual property rights including the protection, licensing or assignment of rights under, or existing by virtue of, a law relating to copyright, design rights, patents or trademarks; activities of employers or an agreement to which employers are party, insofar as it relates to the remuneration, terms or conditions of employment of the employees; activities of trade unions and other associations directed at advancing the terms and conditions of employment of their members and concerted conduct designed to achieve a non-commercial socio-economic objective or similar purpose.

§2. Special Sectors

85. In deciding whether or not section 8 of the Competition and Consumer Protection Act has been breached, it is important to note that the Competition and Consumer Protection Commission need not limit their consideration to whether existing competition will be restricted by the agreement – they will also take into account the possibility that the agreement might affect potential competition in a particular market.

86. It should be noted that in Zambia special sectors are protected. Sector regulated activities in Zambia are fully provided for in sections 42 to 44 of the Competition and Consumer Protection Act.

87. Activities of enterprises in regulated sectors fall under the jurisdiction of the Commission in as far as restrictive business and anticompetitive trade practices are concerned, unless the enterprises fall under the explicit exemption provisions of the Act.

88. The Commission is required under the Competition and Consumer Protection Act to enter into cooperation agreements with sector regulators in the implementation of competition policy and law. Of all the sector regulators in Zambia, four stand out as requiring cooperation with the Commission in the implementation of the country's competition policy and law since they have some competition functions.

89. These are the Pensions and Insurance Authority, the Zambia Information and Communications Technology Authority, the Energy Regulation Board, and the Bank of Zambia. The Commission has negotiated MoUs on concurrent jurisdiction in competition matters with all the sector regulators with competition functions in accordance with the provisions of the Act.

90. The MoU with the energy regulator was signed in September 2011, while that with the ICT regulator was signed in October 2011. The MoUs with the pensions and insurance regulator and with the Bank of Zambia are in the process of finalisation.

§3. State-Owned Enterprises and Public Utilities

91. Section 3(2) of the Competition and Consumer Protection Act binds the State in so far as the State is engaged in commercial activity. While this participation was previously interpreted as applying to 'all economic activities of the State', the new section 3(2) has reversed this by limiting the application only to a market that is open to participation by other enterprises.

92. Whereas the Act does bind the State, it should be noted that section 3(3)(e) of the Competition and Consumer Protection Act provides that the Act shall not apply to the business of any enterprise exercising a statutory monopoly which precludes the entry of another enterprise.

93. This means that statutory monopolies established by an Act of Parliament such as the Zambia Energy Corporation (ZESCO) or Zambia Railways which are defined as commercial undertakings or activities conducted by an entity, whether or not wholly or partly owned by the State, on the basis of statutory provisions that preclude other entities from conducting the same activity, as exempt from the Act.

94. However, the Act does provide that statutory monopolies will only be protected if

- the enterprise does not enter into an agreement that has the purpose of restricting competition;
- the conduct of the enterprise does not, in itself or in conjunction with another enterprise, amount to an abuse of a dominant position; or
- the enterprise, if it wishes to enter into a merger transaction, is in compliance with the provisions of this Act relating to mergers.

§4. Sensible Effect and *De Minimis*

95. The *De Minimis* rule provides that certain agreements that do not have an appreciable or significant impact on competition should not be covered by the Competition and Consumer Protection Act.

96. Although the Act mentions that all restrictive agreements are outlawed, it also provides that the object or effect must be to restrict or distort competition. In some cases some agreements have an insignificant effect and should not be subject to the provisions. Therefore, an agreement falls outside the prohibition … where it has only an insignificant effect on the market, taking into account the weak position which the persons concerned have on the market of the product in question.

97. The rationale for sections 8, 9, 10 and 12 of the Competition and Consumer Protection Act are to outlaw agreements, decisions or concerted practices where competition is sensibly or appreciably restricted. In the *Total Espana SA*[16] case, it was held that the agreement should perceptibly restrict competition within the market for it to be outlawed.

98. It should be noted that the Act provides that all horizontal and vertical agreements per se which means a practice which is prohibited in all circumstances so that it is not necessary for the Commission to demonstrate that it has anticompetitive effects. This implies that these agreements are unlawful in all circumstances and hence the principle of *de minimis* may not apply in Zambia.

99. However, given that section 8 or 9 requires the object or effect to be to distort or restrict competition, it is submitted that *de minimis* does apply, albeit to a very limited extent given the wording in the Competition and Consumer Protection Act.

16. (2009) 5 CMLR 1291.

§5. Cases Where Agreements Containing Contractual Restrictions Will Not Have Anticompetitive Effect

100. Not all contractual restrictions necessarily result in the restriction of competition. In such cases the effect of the restriction was not restrictive or distortionary and thus will escape liability.

101. For example, a contract with a term conferring exclusivity on a distributor might not infringe a provision outlawing restrictive agreements where this seemed to be really necessary for the penetration of a new area by an undertaking.

102. A restrictive agreement may fall outside the ambit of being anticompetitive provided that they are duly limited in time, subject matter and the space it applies to. Put another way, if the agreement is not disproportional, it will meet the requirements of being legal and not be deemed anticompetitive.

103. Other agreements which have been held to not be anticompetitive are those which seek to achieve a commercial objective. In other words, when considering whether an agreement has the effect of restricting competition, it is possible for a party to argue that the restriction was necessary to enable the parties to an agreement to achieve a legitimate commercial purpose and in such circumstances section 8 of the Competition and Consumer Protection Act will not apply.

104. The legitimate commercial purposes that have been identified are the penetration of a new market, the sale of a business or the protection of an essential public service that is provided by a statutory monopoly. Restrictions that are ancillary to a legitimate commercial operation are thereby protected.

§6. Exceptions

105. Sections 18 and 19 of the Competition and Consumer Protection Act recognise that certain other horizontal agreements could be competitively beneficial by fostering efficiencies, promoting international trade, or could be in the public interest, and should therefore not be prohibited per se but should be considered using the rule-of-reason approach.

106. There appears to be an assumption that an agreement that restricts competition by object is incapable of being defended under sections 18 and 19 of the Competition and Consumer Protection Act – but this position is not correct and is simply wrong in law.

107. According to section 19, the Commission shall grant such an exception to such agreements that contribute to or are likely to result in:

– Maintaining or promoting exports from Zambia;

- Promoting or maintaining the efficient production, distribution or provision of goods and services;
- Promoting technical or economic progress in the production, distribution or provision of goods and services;
- Maintaining lower prices, higher quality or greater choice of goods and services for consumers;
- Promoting the competitiveness of micro and small business enterprises in Zambia; or
- Obtaining a benefit for the public which outweighs or would outweigh the lessening in competition that would result, or would be likely to result, from the agreement.

108. Therefore, even an agreement that has as its *object* the restriction of competition in the sense of sections 8, 9, 10 or 12 off the Competition and Consumer Protection Act is capable, in principle, of satisfying one of the conditions laid down in section 19 of the Act and applies for such exception to apply.

109. An enterprise that wishes to be exempted from a prohibition under the Act may apply to the Commission for exemption in the prescribed manner and form upon payment of the prescribed fee and demonstrating they meet on of the criteria mentioned above.

110. The Commission may grant an exemption subject to such conditions and for such period as it considers appropriate. Where conditions are attached to an exception, an enterprise that does not comply with a condition of an exemption is liable to pay the Commission a fine not exceeding 10% of its annual turnover.

111. The Commission shall, where it refuses to grant an exemption, inform the applicant accordingly and give the reasons therefor.

112. The Commission may amend an exemption granted under section 19, if some other enterprise has succeeded to the interest in the enterprise exempted, by substituting the name of the enterprise with the name of the successor; the name of the enterprise has changed, by substituting the name so changed; or there has been a change in market circumstances since the exemption was granted.

113. The Commission may revoke an exemption, if the exemption was granted on materially incorrect or misleading information; there has been a material change of circumstances since the exemption was granted; or the enterprise exempted fails to comply with any condition upon which the exemption was granted.

114. The Commission shall, where it proposes to revoke an exemption as above, give notice, in writing, of the proposed action to the enterprise to which the exemption was granted and request the enterprise to submit to the Commission, within seven days of the receipt of the notice, any representation which the enterprise may wish to make on the proposed action.

§7. STATUTORY MONOPOLIES

115. There are two forms of parastatal organisations are identifiable in Zambia: those which are created by specific Acts of Parliament also known as statutory corporations or boards and those established by registration under the Companies Act.[17] These statutory organisations are controlled from respective line ministries through their boards of directors. These include such entities as the State Lotteries Board,[18] the Diary Produce Board (DPB)[19], the Development Bank of Zambia (DBZ),[20] the National Savings and Credit Bank,[21] the Zambia National Tourist Board,[22] the Bank of Zambia[23] and the Zambia National Building Society.[24]

116. Statutory corporations are used chiefly as entities through which specific public services are undertaken or provided while realising a profit. Perhaps the best distinction between these two kinds of parastatals is to be found in the categorisation given in the Mwanakatwe Commission Report on Parastatals. The Commission used two different terms to identify parastatals, namely, statutory corporations and state-controlled companies. It defined a statutory corporation as:

> 'The body corporate established by statute with defined powers and duties in some specified area of action and subject to the control of a particular Minister who may give directions as to the conduct of its affairs. The nature of the organization can only be changed if its governing statute is amended or repealed and replaced.'

117. The same report explains what a state-controlled company is in the following terms:

> The company limited by shares and incorporated under the provisions of the Companies Act, cap 686 of the laws of Zambia. It is the sole or majority interest by the State which distinguishes this type of parastatal from any other limited company and in legal terms, its structure is exactly the same as that of its purely private counterpart. Its operations are governed by its Memorandum and Articles of Association, by the provisions of the Companies Act and by the decisions of its board. The direct shareholding of the Government varies but is 100 per cent in the case of the main controlling groups.

17. Chapter 388 of the laws of Zambia.
18. Chapter 328 of the laws of Zambia.
19. Chapter 230 of the laws of Zambia. The Dairy Industry Development Act 22 of 2010 repealed and replaced this Act.
20. Chapter 398 of the laws of Zambia.
21. Chapter 423 of the laws of Zambia.
22. Established under the Tourism Act Ch. 155 of the laws of Zambia.
23. Chapter 360 of the laws of Zambia.
24. Established under the Building Societies Act Ch. 412 of the laws of Zambia.

118. The establishment of parastatal organisations in Zambia is an interesting example of how the political, social and economic climate in any country can dictate either the content or the interpretation of the law. A meaningful explanation of the law relating to parastatal companies in Zambia as commercial entities calls for the examination, no matter how undesirable this may be, of the economic politics of the country following independence in 1964. One is justified to state that the political climate had a lot to do with the economic direction which the country took, characterised by the serious involvement of the state in the running of business through parastatal organisations.

119. It should be noted that under section 3(e) of the Competition and Consumer Protection Act, the business of any enterprise exercising a statutory monopoly, which precludes the entry of another enterprise into the relevant market in Zambia is excluded from the application of the Act due largely to then nature of the public benefit the service and goods they provide are.

120. For the purpose of section 3(e) of the Competition and Consumer Protection Act only applied to the first type of statutory monopolies, those established by an Act of Parliament and not those that are incorporated in terms of the Companies Act.

121. Following the privatisation of the parastatal sector in Zambia, many state-owned or controlled business entities in various sectors remained operational in one form or another under a direct reporting arrangement to line Ministries. Permanent secretaries of line Ministries continued to sit on the board of directors for purposes of monitoring and policy guidance. This was somewhat disconcerting particularly given the manner in which government detachment from business was envisioned in the dawn to multiparty politics. Granted the actual difficulties encountered during the privatisation process, the continued existence or reincarnation of state ownership of business entities appeared an unlikely prospect.

122. The truth, however, is that even after the ambitious privatisation process itself, and the virtual demise of the conglomerate ZIMCO and other once dynamic state corporations notably INDECO and FINDECO in the 1990s, Ministries remain ill equipped to direct commercial enterprise. They do not wherewithal in the nature of commercial and investment know-how and resources to ensure positive performance of these business entities. Political interference continues to be the order of the day. One of the consequences is that these enterprises have been unable to give government a return on its investment and contribute to the Treasury by way of dividends and taxes.

123. The phased approach of the privatisation process under which the sale of equity in parastatal companies was done in tranches somewhat gave room for more deliberate reflection on the immediate and medium-term consequences of the privatisation programme. In fact, angst, disappointment and regret in many cases consumed sections of the public in the period following privatisation. Many jobs were lost when new buyers of formerly state-owned businesses restructured these companies, involving in many instances, downsizing of the work force or the realignment of business. Some new owners of formerly state-owned businesses dismantled equipment in established manufacturing factories and shipped it out of the country.

124. One of the policy initiatives of the Patriotic Front Government as enshrined in its 2011–2016 Manifesto was the creation of INDECO. This was to be used as a vehicle through which the government was to deepen and support the country's industrialisation so as to create jobs and reduce poverty. The intention was clearly that government would continue to participate as a co-investor alongside private enterprise.

125. On 20 September 2013, government announced its desire to restructure and improve the system for supervision and control of parastatals to ensure their enhanced contribution to the reduction of unemployment and economic development.[25] Later, Cabinet sanctioned the launch of the IDC and the transfer of government interest in all state-owned enterprises incorporated under the Companies Act from the Ministry of Finance to the IDC. The latter was henceforth to hold the shares on behalf of government in state-owned enterprises. Cabinet also approved the creation of a Sovereign Wealth Fund to safeguard the interest of posterity.[26]

126. The IDC incorporated in early 2014 an investment company wholly owned by the Zambian government through the Minister of Finance who, under the Minister of Finance (Incorporation) Act Chapter 349 of the Laws of Zambia, is a body corporate. Its mandate is to facilitate provision and raising of long-term finance for projects and to serve as an investment holding company for state-owned enterprises and new investments that would eventually generate earnings for the Sovereign Wealth Fund.

127. INDECO is now a shareholder and investor in sectors that include agriculture, forestry, manufacturing, financial services, mining, energy, telecommunications, logistics, medical, education, tourism, real estate and media.

128. Its portfolio of companies across sectors include Nanga Farms Limited, Zambia Forestry and Forest Industries Corporation, NIEC Business School, Afrox Zambia Limited Indeni Petroleum Refinery Limited, Zambia Electricity Supply Corporation, Indo-Zambia Bank Limited, Zambia State Insurance Corporation, Zambia National Commercial Bank Plc, Times Printpak Zambia Limited, Zambia Daily Mail Limited, Zambia Education Publishing House Limited, Zambia Printing Company, Zamtel Limited, Engineering Services Corporation, Lusaka South Multi-Facility Economic Zone Limited, Mulungushi Textiles Limited, Mupepetwe Development Company, Nitrogen Chemicals of Zambia Limited, Zamcapitol Enterprises Limited, Lusaka Trust Hospital, Medical Stores Limited, Kagem Minerals Limited,

25. President Michael Sata made the announcement at the Official Opening of the 3rd session of the 11th National Assembly.
26. At its thirty-second meeting held on 16 Dec. 2013.

Kariba Minerals Limited, ZCCM Investment Holdings Plc., Mulungushi Village Complex Limited, Mukuba Hotel Limited, Mulungushi International Conference Centre, Zambia International Trade Fair, Mpulungu Harbour Corporation Limited, Zambia Airways (2014) Limited, and Zambia Railways Limited.

129. A worrisome feature of the IDC concerns its corporate governance. The Board of Directors which provides overall guidance and direction in the management of the company's assets and investments is made up of three Cabinet Ministers, namely those responsible for Finance, Commerce Trade and Industry, and Agriculture. It also has two mainstream civil servants: The Secretary to the Treasury and the Permanent Secretary for Commerce Trade and Industry. There are then seven private sector members and three Executive Directors of the IDC acting as ex officio members. The Republican President is the Chairman of the Board. The President appoints and dismisses Board members. In addition to the ordinary fiduciary duties to the company, the IDC Board is also accountable to the President.

130. It is expected that IDC will publish its annual reports bearing its group financial accounts and portfolio performance. It will also declare dividends to its shareholder.

Chapter 3. Overview of Substantive Provisions

§1. Restrictive Agreements Generally

131. Section 8 of the Competition and Consumer Protection Act provides that

> Any category of agreement, decision or concerted practice which has as its object or effect, the prevention, restriction or distortion of competition to an appreciable extent in Zambia is anticompetitive and prohibited.

132. The provision makes it very clear that agreements, decisions or concerted practices that have the object or effect of seeking to prevent or restrict or distort competition are prohibited.

133. The Act defines an agreement as any form of agreement, whether or not legally enforceable, between enterprises which is implemented or intended to be implemented in Zambia and includes an oral agreement or a decision by a trade association or an association of enterprises. Under Zambian Competition Law, the Act recognises two kinds of restrictive agreements, namely horizontal and vertical agreements. These two kinds of agreements will be dealt with in turn.

134. In relation to a concerted practice, section 3 of the Competition and Consumer Protection Act defines these as a practice which involves some form of communication or coordination between competitors falling short of an actual agreement but which replaces their independent action and restricts or lessens competition between them.

135. However, it is important to note that whereas the State and bodies exercising statutory functions are subject to Competition Law and the Competition and Consumer Protection Act, there are some exceptions. First, section 3(3)(e) of the Competition and Consumer Protection Act provides that the Act shall not apply to the business of any enterprise exercising a statutory monopoly which precludes the entry of another enterprise. The most common statutory monopoly in Zambia is the Zambia Energy Corporation (ZESCO) – in such an instance, this entity is not subject to the provisions on restrictive agreements.

136. Second, activities of enterprises that are exempt in terms of the Competition and Consumer Protection Act are not subject the provisions on restrictive agreements. In Zambia these relate energy, the banking sector, pension and communications. These fall under the following statutory agencies namely, the Pensions and Insurance Authority, the Zambia Information and Communications Technology Authority, the Energy Regulation Board, and the Bank of Zambia.

137. The Commission has negotiated MoUs on concurrent jurisdiction in competition matters with all the sector regulators with competition functions in accordance with the provisions of the Act.

138. The Commission may, at any time, during or after an investigation under this Part, enter into a consent agreement with an enterprise under investigation or request the enterprise to give an undertaking in the prescribed manner and form.

139. The Commission may, where a restrictive agreement falls within the scope of sections 8,9, 10 or 12 considers appropriate to ensure that the enterprise ceases to be a party to the restrictive agreement.

140. Such a direction may require an enterprise to terminate or modify the restrictive agreement concerned within such period as may be specified by the Commission.

141. Further, in addition to, or instead of, giving a direction, the Competition and Consumer Protection Commission may make an order imposing a financial penalty on the enterprise not exceeding 10% of that enterprise's annual turnover during the period of the breach of the prohibition up to a maximum period of five years.

142. Section 58 (1) and (3) of the Competition Act state that:

(1) The Commission may, where a restrictive agreement falls within the scope of sections eight, nine, ten and twelve, give an enterprise such directions, in writing, as the Commission considers appropriate to ensure that the enterprise ceases to be a party to the restrictive agreement.
(2) A direction under subsection (1) may, in particular, require an enterprise to terminate or modify the restrictive agreement concerned within such period as may be specified by the Commission.
(3) The Commission may, in relation to a restrictive agreement referred to under subsection (1), in addition to, or instead of, giving a direction, make an order imposing a financial penalty on the enterprise not exceeding 10 percent of that enterprise's annual turnover during the period of the breach of the prohibition up to a maximum period of five years.

143. The law as provided in section 58 (3) of the Competition Act is clear and unambiguous that a fine imposed by the Respondent where it finds a breach of sections 8, 9, 10 and 12 of the Competition Act cannot exceed 10% of an enterprise's annual turnover during the period of the breach.

144. Section 58 (4) of the Competition Act which provides that

> the Commission shall not impose a financial penalty unless it is satisfied that the breach of the prohibition was committed intentionally or negligently.

145. Therefore, the Commission shall not impose a financial penalty unless it is satisfied that the breach of the prohibition was committed intentionally or negligently. An order imposing a penalty shall be in writing and shall specify the date by which the penalty is required to be paid.

146. The Competition and Consumer Protection Tribunal had the opportunity to interpret section 58(4) of the Competition Act in the case of *MRI Seed Zambia*. In that case, the Tribunal held that in relation to intention:

> Intention to do an act signifies mens rea, a mental state in which one deliberately violates the law … evidence of one's state of mind is difficult to assess, especially if that person has not shown any manifestation or overt evidence of the person's state of mind. Accordingly, courts will thus, often have to infer subjective purpose i.e., where the gist of the offense is in the intent, there must be also some act in the direction of such intent.

147. Based on the above definition of intention when interpreting section 58(4) of the Act, the subjective intention of the Appellant was never to create an environment where members could not compete. This is clear from the documentation alluded to above. Furthermore, in the *MRI Seed Zambia* case, the Tribunal held that where a party is transparent, intent cannot be attributed to their conduct.

148. In relation to negligence, the court in *MRI Seed Zambia* provided guidance when they held that in relation to negligence:

> The word 'negligently' as used in section 37 of the Act connotes objective mens rea. In terms of objective mens rea one need not intend to commit a wrongful act, but that act need only fall below objective standards of behaviour, i.e., a wrongful act that falls below objective standards of behaviour will, without regard to the offender's subjective mental state at the time of the commission of that act, be punished. Negligent acts would fall in this category.

149. The tribunal in *MRI Seed Zambia* held that in interpreting negligence, the conduct must fall below the standard of the ordinary person. The holding in the case was to the effect that ignorance of the law was a defence and the fact that the local counsel in that case did not review the transaction indicated that parties in that case were not negligent.

150. Where the Commission determines, after review, that an enterprise is a party to a restrictive agreement referred to under sections 8, 9, 10 or 12, the Commission may in terms of section 59 of the Competition and Consumer Protection Act provide that in relation to the restrictive agreement, the agreement has the object or effect of preventing, restricting or distorting competition, the Commission may give the enterprise such directions as it considers necessary, reasonable and practicable to:

(a) remedy, mitigate or prevent the adverse effects on competition that the Commission has identified; or
(b) remedy, mitigate or prevent any detrimental effects on users and consumers so far as they have resulted from, or are likely to result from, the adverse effects on, or the absence of, competition.

151. Where the parties to a horizontal agreement, together supply or acquire 30% or more of goods or services of any description. in a relevant market in Zambia; or a vertical agreement, individually supply or acquire, at either one of the two levels of the market that are linked by the agreement, 15% or more of goods or services of any description in a relevant market in Zambia; the parties shall apply to the Commission for authorisation of the agreement in the prescribed manner and form. The Commission shall, upon receipt of an application under subsection (1), carry out an investigation to determine whether the agreement is prohibited under the Competition and Consumer Protection. Act.

§2. Dominant Undertakings

152. In Zambia, an enterprise shall refrain from any act or conduct if, through abuse or acquisition of a dominant position of market power, the act or conduct limits access to markets or otherwise unduly restrains competition, or has or is likely to have adverse effect on trade or the economy in general.

153. The Competition and Consumer Protection Act defines a dominant position as a situation where an enterprise or a group of enterprises possesses such economic strength in a market as to make it possible for it to operate in that market, and to adjust prices or output, without effective constraint from competitors or potential competitors.

154. More specifically, section 15 of the Competition and Consumer Protection Act provides that a dominant position exists in relation to the supply of goods or services in Zambia, if 30% or more of those goods or services are supplied or acquired by one enterprise; or 60% or more of those goods or services are supplied or acquired by not more than three enterprises.

155. A finding of dominance involves a two-stage assessment. First, there is a need to properly define the relevant market is a necessary precondition for any application for the provision outlawing dominance and abuse of that dominance. Having defined the relevant market, it is necessary to determine whether an undertaking has a dominant position in that market. This cannot be determined purely by reference to an undertaking's market share.

156. Section 15 of the Competition and Consumer Protection Act clearly assists us in fulfilling the two stage assessment by helping us deduce what dominance is in the Zambian context. The provision provides that a dominant position exists in relation to the supply of goods or services in Zambia, if 30% or more of those goods or services are supplied or acquired by one enterprise; or 60% or more of those goods or services are supplied or acquired by not more than three enterprises.

157. The first leg of the definition in section 15 of the Competition and Consumer Protection Act focuses on market share which is a very important consideration. In *Hoffmann-La Roche* the Court of Justice pointed out that:

> A substantial market share as evidence of the existence of a dominant position is not a constant factor and its importance varies from market to market according to the structure of these markets, especially as far as production, supply and demand are concerned.

158. Market shares provide a useful first indication of the market structure and of the relative importance of the undertakings active on it. An assessment of market power requires that market conditions generally be taken into account, including the dynamics of the market, the extent to which products are differentiated and the trend or development of market shares over time.

159. The author submits that whereas the definition in the Act is welcome, it is unduly narrow and limited to the market position and buying power in one context. It is submitted that when crafting the definition of dominance, wider consideration should have been considered such as constraints imposed by the existing supplies from, and the position on the market of, actual competitors (the market position of the dominant undertaking and its competitors), constraints imposed by the credible threat of future expansion by actual competitors or entry by potential competitors (expansion and entry) and constraints imposed by the bargaining strength of the undertaking's customers (countervailing buyer power).

160. The above is important because in established case such as *United Brands*, the courts have held that firms with lower market share may be dominant if other factors are considered. Thus, whereas market share and supply is important, other considerations such as the absence of any competitive constraint or market share was considerably larger than that of any other individual competitor may also show dominance. For example, if an enterprise in Zambia has 25% market share it won't be considered dominant in terms of section 15 of the Zambian Competition and Consumer Protection Act even if its market share is far much larger than any other competitor.

161. The focus on market share is unadvisable because market shares do not in themselves determine whether a firm has a dominant position; in particular they cannot indicate the competitive pressure exerted by firms not yet operating on the market but with the capacity to enter it in a timely manner.

162. Other factors such the importance of the impact of expansion by existing competitors and limited entry by potential ones to market also indicate dominance. Such barriers include legal barriers; economic advantages enjoyed by the dominant undertaking; costs and network effects that impede customers from switching from one supplier to another; and the dominant firm's own conduct and performance could affect the determination of a dominant position. This underscores the fact the focus on market share in section 15 of the Competition and Consumer Protection Act may have been misguided.

163. The economic performance of an undertaking may be a factor indicating dominance. Further, the court in *United Brands* case agreed with the idea that the conduct of a firm could be taken into account in deciding whether it is dominant. This means, for example, that it might be legitimate to take into account the fact that a firm has offered discriminatory rebates to certain customers in deciding whether it is dominant: the rebates may themselves prevent competitors entering the market and so constitute a barrier to entry. This further shows that market share is not the only consideration in determining dominance.

164. The threshold for establishing the existence of dominant position has been lowered from the old Act's 50% of production or distribution of goods or services in Zambia, or any substantial part of the country, to 30% in the current Competition and Consumer Protection Act.

165. It is noted that the new dominance threshold of 30% is rather low, and goes against the practice of higher thresholds that has been established in the region. Competition legislation in other jurisdictions in the region does not provide for a strict dominance threshold, but experience has shown that this gives the competition authority discretion in determining dominance, A mixture of a rebuttable presumption of dominance and a strict threshold, as in South Africa, would seem appropriate.

166. Another problem is that whereas the Act does give guidelines on what constitutes a dominant position and what a dominant position could entail, further analysis is required to deduce if a company with a dominant position (30%) or more of those goods or services are supplied or acquired by one enterprise; or (60% or more of those goods or services are supplied or acquired by not more than three enterprises) has abused its dominant position in line with section 16(2).

167. As elucidated above, enterprises in Zambia are not permitted to carry on business in any manner that amounts to abuse off a dominant position of market power. Section 16(2) of the Competition and Consumer Protection Act provides that abuse of a dominant position includes:

- imposing, directly or indirectly, unfair purchase or selling prices or other unfair trading conditions;
- limiting or restricting production, market outlets or market access, investment, technical development or technological progress in a manner that affects competition;
- applying dissimilar conditions to equivalent transactions with other trading parties;
- making the conclusion of contracts subject to acceptance by other parties of supplementary conditions which by their nature or according to commercial usage have no connection with the subject matter of the contracts;
- denying any person access to an essential facility;
- charging an excessive price to the detriment of consumers; or
- selling goods below their marginal or variable cost.

168. Where the Zambia Competition Commission may review a merger of two or more entities falls below the prescribed threshold for authorisation if they have reasonable grounds to believe that the merger is likely to create a position of dominance in a localised product or geographical market or the merger is likely to contribute to the creation of a dominant position through a series of acquisitions which are not individually subject to prior notification.

§3. CONCENTRATIONS

169. It is important to understand that the expression 'merger' as used in competition policy includes a far broader range of corporate transactions than full mergers of this kind.

170. Where A acquires all, or a majority of, the shares in B, this would be described as a merger if it results in A being able to control the strategic business decisions of B; even the acquisition of a minority shareholding may be sufficient, in particular circumstances, to qualify as a merger.

171. The question is whether A will acquire 'the possibility of exercising decisive influence' over the strategic commercial behaviour of B the question is whether A would at least have 'material influence' over B.

172. The acquisition of assets – for example a well-known brand name – can amount to a merger. Two or more undertakings which merge part of their businesses into a newly established joint venture company, may be found to be parties to a merger. In each case the essential question is whether previously independent businesses have come or will come under common control with the consequence that, in the future, the market will function less competitively than it did prior to the merger.

173. For the sake of convenience, the term 'merger' and concentrations will be used in this and the following chapters to encompass all these phenomena unless the context requires a different usage.

§4. OTHER PROHIBITIONS

174. Section 12 of the Competition and Consumer Protection Act provides that subject to section 8 which deals with restrictive agreements generally, section 9 which deals with horizontal agreements and section 10 which deal with vertical agreements, an agreement between enterprises is prohibited if the Commission determines that the agreement has the effect of preventing, distorting or. restricting competition or substantially lessening competition in a market for any goods or services in Zambia; and the agreement is not exempted under section 19 of the Competition and Consumer Protection Act.

175. A person who, or an enterprise which commits any of the following is liable to pay the Commission a fine not exceeding 10% of that person's or enterprise's annual turnover or 150,000 penalty units, whichever is higher.

(a) falsely represents that:
  (i) any goods are of a particular standard, quality, value, grade, composition, style or model or have a particular history or previous use;
  (ii) any services are of a particular standard, quality, value or grade;
  (iii) any goods are new;
  (iv) a particular person has agreed to acquire goods or services; or
  (v) any goods or services have sponsorship, approval, affiliation, performance characteristics, accessories, uses or benefits that they do not have; or

(b) makes a false or misleading representation concerning:
  (i) the price of any goods or services;
  (ii) the availability of facilities for the repair of any goods or of spare parts for goods;
  (iii) the place of origin of any goods;
  (iv) the need for any goods or services; or
  (v) the existence, exclusion or effect of any condition, warranty, guarantee, right or remedy;

176. A person or an enterprise shall not supply a consumer with goods that are defective, not fit for the purpose for which they are normally used or for the purpose that the consumer indicated to the person or the enterprise.

177. A product that is sold in Zambia shall have a label to clearly indicate the product name, the ingredients used in the product, the date of manufacture and expiry of the product, the manufacturer's name, the physical location of the manufacturer, the telephone number and any other contact details of the manufacturer. A person or an enterprise shall not sell any goods to consumers unless the goods conform to the mandatory consumer product information standard for the class of goods set by the Zambia Bureau of Standards or other relevant competent body.

178. A person or an enterprise shall not sell any goods to consumers unless the goods conform to the mandatory safety standard for the class of goods set by the Zambia Bureau of Standards or other relevant competent body.

179. In a contract between an enterprise and a consumer, the contract or a term of the contract shall be regarded as unfair if it causes a significant imbalance in the parties' rights and obligations arising under the contract, to the detriment of the consumer.

180. A person or an enterprise shall not charge a consumer more than the price indicated or displayed on a product or service.

§5. TESTS OF ILLEGALITY

181. An agreement is illegal if it contravenes the Competition and Consumer Protection Act, any other piece of Zambian legislation or the common law. The Supreme Court of Zambia recently confirmed in the case of *Hiteshbhai Patel v Agyen-Frempong Kofi and Agyen-Frempong Osei*[27] that parties to a contract should be presumed to contemplate a legal rather than an illegal course of proceedings when contracting. This notwithstanding, the law provides guidance on what occurs when a contract is illegal.

182. In the seminal case of *Mohamed S Itowala v. Variety Bureau de Change*[28] the Supreme Court of Zambia provided that a contract can be illegal in two ways:

- illegal at formation; and
- contracts that are illegally performed.

183. First, a contract can be illegal in its formation which means that when it was formed or created, it was contrary to the law. In other words, the contract is illegal at the time it is formed. These contracts cannot be performed in accordance with their terms without the commission of an illegal act. Therefore, illegality may also exist in regard to the making and/or purpose of the contract when it was formed.

184. The second instance from the *Mohamed S Itowala v. Variety Bureau de Change*[29] case is that a contract can also be illegal based on the manner in which it is to be performed. Illegality may exist in regard to the performance, as in a contract to perform an illegal operation; or the consideration itself may be illegal.

185. A contract may be created legitimately but become illegal and therefore unenforceable because the manner in which it is performed is illegal. The illegality as to performance may arise because either both or one of the parties may intend to perform the contract in an illegal manner.

186. Where a contract is to do an act which cannot be performed without a violation of the law, it is void and without legal effect, whether the parties knew the law or not. This rule also applies where an Act of Parliament makes the contract illegal: the parties' ignorance of the law does not make it legal – it will still be without any legal effect.

187. However, the situation is different where the contract is not unlawful in that it is capable of performance in a lawful way and both parties contemplate that it may

27. SCZ Appeal No. 13/2017.
28. SCZ Judgment No. 15 of 2001.
29. SCZ Judgment No. 15 of 2001.

be performed in an unlawful way. In that case the contract may be enforced provided it is shown there was never an intention to carry out the contract in an unlawful manner after they discovered the contract contemplated an unlawful act, and at least the party seeking to enforce the contract can carry it out in a legal manner.

188. The law in relation to an agreement which is contrary to statute or regulations was aptly summarised in the case of *Mohamed S Itowala v. Variety Bureau de Change.*[30] The Supreme Court held that:

> In this particular case even assuming that the plaintiff was aware of the illegality and was trying to perform an illegal contract, the illegality would only have been in respect of the excess 5,000 dollars and not the entire amount of money. But in fact there was no occasion to assume that the appellant intended an illegal way of doing anything. It was clearly a misdirection to find that there was any question of anyone trying to defraud anyone else when the plaintiff applied to buy dollars.

189. The Supreme Court held that the money he paid was not irrecoverable, and he had a clear title to the money, which should have been paid back to him. The Supreme Court in *Mohamed S Itowala v. Variety Bureau de Change*[31] held that it would not be permissible for the other party to the transaction to benefit from the alleged illegality by keeping the money.

190. The general rule with regard to illegal contracts is that a court will not assist a party to enforce an illegal contract or, as the Supreme Court put it in the *Gideon Mundanda v. Timothy Mulwani and The Agricultural Finance Co Ltd and Mwiinga*[32] case, condone the flouting of the law.

191. An illegal contract is void, and consequently, the court will not assist a party to such an agreement either directly or indirectly: *ex turpi causa non oritur actio* – the action arises on a base cause. Accordingly, as a general rule, no money or goods delivered under such a contract can be recovered by action.

192. The Zambian Supreme Court in the case of *Itowala* provided four instances where neither party can sue upon an illegal contract. The four instances provided are if:

(a) both knew that it necessarily involved the commission of an act which, to their knowledge, is legally objectionable, that is illegal or otherwise against public policy, or
(b) both knew that the contract is intended to be performed in a manner which, to their knowledge is legally objectionable in that sense, or

30. SCZ Judgment No. 15 of 2001.
31. SCZ Judgment No. 15 of 2001.
32. (1987) ZR 29 (SC).

(c) the purpose of the contract is legally objectionable and that purpose is shared by both parties, or
(d) both participate in performing the contract in a manner which they know to be legally objectionable.

193. Based on the above, if both parties knew that the contract was illegal or intended to be performed in an illegal manner, neither party can claim relief. Where one party is unaware of the illegality then they may have remedies available, including recovery of any money handed over in advance of the contract. If a party goes on with the contract with the knowledge of what is objectionable, they cannot recover anything.

194. Where statute or the common law has declared that a class of contract will be illegal if made then such a contract can never be legally formed or performed and will be illegal from the moment of formation. There are then a number of consequences for such agreements. Since the contract is illegal it is also unenforceable by either party.

195. The party or claimant may be able to recover money paid or property transferred under an illegal contract if he can establish his right to the money or the property without relying on the illegal contract.

196. Where the contract is capable of being performed legally, the court will uphold it. In *Golf Consultancy and Tourism Limited v. Chainama Hills Golf Club Limited*[33] the Supreme Court of Zambia dealt with a contract for the sale of land for USD 6 000 000 or its Zambia Kwacha equivalent. At the time there was a law in place that prohibited quoting or selling goods or services of a domestic nature in foreign currency. The Supreme Court held that:

> If a contract can be performed legally, then we must encourage such performance particularly in this case, where the contract was not illegal as to formation.

197. The Supreme Court provided that although the contract was illegal at formation, it was capable of being performed legally in that the purchase price of the land could be paid in local Zambian currency.

198. Where money or goods have passed under an illegal contract contrary to the Competition and Consumer Protection Act or any other law, the defendant is in a stronger position than the plaintiff who seeks the aid of the court to recover his property. Because the court usually refuses its aid once it discovers the illegality, the defendant to whom goods have been delivered or money has been paid may sometimes keep the goods or money. The maxim applied is in *pari delicto potior est conditio defendentis*, which is where there is equal wrongdoing, the position of the defendant is stronger.

33. SCZ Appeal No. 162/2014.

199. The common law provides an exception to this rule. It provides that where the party seeking recovery is not *in pari delicto*, i.e., is not as culpable as the other party, then they shall be entitled to claim relief. The same is true where the illegality is not vital to the cause, property or money can be recovered, the same can be recovered.

200. Where work done has been done under a void or illegal contract, the injured party cannot recover damages for breach, because no contract exists, but they may recover on a *quantum meruit* basis In *Rating Valuation Consortium and D W Zyambo & Associates (suing as a firm) v. The Lusaka City Council and the Zambia National Tender Board,*[34] the Zambian Supreme Court held that where one accepts the fruits of another's labour, in circumstances where payment would be expected, he must pay for it.

201. As such, the Supreme Court held that the party could recover a *quantum meruit* as reasonable costs incurred in preparation to undertake the contract. The Supreme Court held that one cannot seek shelter in the doctrine of illegality to avoid paying reasonable costs incurred by another to the contract even though the contract is illegal either at formation or in performance. The Supreme court held that even where *quantum meruit* is not pleaded, a party is not debarred from being entitled to this sum in a claim before the courts if the claim warrants such an award, confirming the position in *DP Services Limited v. Municipal Council of Kabwe*.[35]

202. In Evolution Group Limited v. Pan African Building Society,[36] the Court of Appeal per Chishimba JA held that:

> The principle of *quantum meruit* applied in instances where work has been carried out under a contract which for one reason or another, is unenforceable, void or illegal. We refer to a passage from Halsbury's Laws of England 4th Edition, Volume 9, where the learned authors state that: In some circumstances, a plaintiff may, recover on a quantum meruit in respect of work done under a contract which is unenforceable, void or illegal … where work done at the request of the defendant and of which he has the benefit, the plaintiff can recover on a quantum meruit. Where a contract is void as being made without authority, a plaintiff who has rendered services under it may, be entitled to recover on a quantum meruit.

203. The Court of Appeal then went on to provide that quantum meruit is a reasonable price to be paid for work actually done or goods actually supplied pursuant to an illegal, void or unenforceable contract. In the circumstances of this case, the principle of quantum meruit was inapplicable.

---

34. SCZ Judgment No. 13 of 2004.
35. (1976) ZR 110.
36. CAZ Appeal No. 2/2019.

204. Sometimes a contract contrary to competition law is illegal as to part only. In appropriate circumstances, an illegal or void part of a contract may be severed by taking out the objectionable part, enabling that which remains to be enforced. In these circumstances, the court may divide the contract, enforcing the valid portion and refusing assistance in regard to the illegal part.

205. There are three main forms of severance: severance associated with dealing,[37] severance of an objectionable promise,[38] and severance of an objectionable part of the term of the contract.[39]

I. Per Se Prohibitions and Naked Restraints

206. A per se prohibition or naked restraint is one that is explicitly anticompetitive in nature, and has the object or effect of seeking to distort or restrict competition. These restraints have no objective or commercial justification and are not eligible to be excluded from the application of the Act in terms of section 19 of the Act.

207. These agreements are patently unlawful and will not be enforced. The Competition and Consumer Protection. Act provides that per se in relation to a prohibited practice, means a practice which is prohibited in all circumstances so that it is not necessary for the Commission to demonstrate that it has anticompetitive effects.

II. Balancing Tests

208. For a restrictive agreement to be deemed void and without effect, it must have the 'object or effect' of restricting or distorting competition. This section will consider the balancing test that goes into assessing if this criteria is met.

209. In the case of *MRI Seed Zambia and Others v. Amiran Zambia Limited,*[40] the Competition and Consumer Protection Tribunal held that:

> As for the meaning of the text of section 8 of the Act, we find it necessary to point out that the object and effect envisaged are couched in the terms 'has as its object or effect'. This means this is not qualified so as to be the 'object or effect of solely'. Therefore, the object or effect with which section 8 statute is concerned with could be of many. Therefore, unless the statute specifically

37. *Amoco Australia v. Rocca Bros Motor Engineering Co* (1973) HCA 40; 133 CLR; 1 ALR 385.
38. *Brooks v. Burns Philp Trustee* (1969) HCA 4; 121 CLR 432; (1969) ALR 321.
39. *Bacchus Marsh Concentrated Milk Co v. Joseph Nathan & Co* (1919) HCA 18; 26 CLR 410.
40. Appeal No. 2017/CCPT/001/CON.

grants a leeway by way of exception or justification, an agreement is captured by the section simply by measurement on an objective standard in terms of the competition mischief.

210. From the above, this Honourable Tribunal stated the object or effect of an agreement, decision or concerted practice need not have been the sole object of preventing, restricting or distorting competition. The Tribunal provided that even where certain conduct has multiple objects or effect, the Tribunal is only concerned if the conduct has some object or have effect on competition. What is critical in determining whether the conduct is anticompetitive is whether one of the objects or effects of the conduct is to restrict or distort competition, notwithstanding the existence of other objectives or effects.

A. *Effect*

211. As it relates to deducing the effect of an agreement, the Tribunal in *Insurance Association of Zambia and Others v. The Competition and Consumer Protection Commission* stated that it should be considered whether the resolution had the effect of restricting competition by impact or effect on other traders or enterprises in the same industry. The Tribunal further guided that determining the effect of an agreement requires examining the agreement within the factual and legal context and effect on the market.

212. Effect relates to agreements that have as their effect the restriction of competition. Therefore, it must be borne in mind that in assessing an agreement… account should be taken of the actual conditions in which it functions, in particular the economic context in which the undertaking operate, the products or services covered by the agreement and the actual structure of the market concerned … unless it is an agreement containing obvious restrictions of competition such as price-fixing, market-sharing or the control of outlets … In the latter case, such restrictions may be weighed against their claimed pro-competitive effects only in the context of (a provision that provides for exceptions – which in provided for under section 18 to 21 of the Zambian Competition and Consumer Protection Act)

213. Where it is not possible to say that the object of an agreement is to restrict competition, it is necessary to conduct an extensive analysis of its effect on the market before it can be found to infringe section 8 of the Competition and Consumer Protection Act.

B. Object

214. The first step is therefore to deduce the precise object of the agreement. We have to consider what is the 'object' test contemplated by section 8 of the Competition and Consumer Protection Act. As the Competition Act itself does not elaborate on the meaning of *'object'*, ineluctably, we have to have recourse to judicial interpretation.

215. In *Insurance Association of Zambia and Others v. The Competition and Consumer Protection Commission*, the Competition and Consumer Protection Tribunal stated that in considering the 'object' of an agreement, recourse needs to be made to judicial interpretation as the Act does not provide a definition. The Tribunal stated that 'to establish the object of a particular agreement, it is necessary to take into consideration the objectives and economic context as well as the content of the provisions', and the test is an objective standard.

216. In the Zambian decision of *MRI Seed Zambia and Others v. Amiran Zambia Limited,*[41] it was stated that in order to decide whether an agreement restricts competition as its object:

> … regard must be had inter alia to the context of its provisions, the objectives it seeks to attain and the economic and legal context of which it forms part.

217. In in order to ascribe an anticompetitive object to a concerted practice, it is enough or sufficient that it had the potential to have a negative impact on competition: the effects of such a practice would be relevant only to the level of any fine or the award of damages to victims of the harm.

218. Furthermore, in order to find a restriction by object, it was not necessary to demonstrate a direct effect on prices to end users. Section 8 of the Competition and Consumer Protection Act is designed to protect the structure of the market and competition as such.

219. The word 'object' in the context of section 8 of the Competition and Consumer Protection Act does not mean the subjective intention of the parties when entering into the agreement, but the objective meaning and purpose of the agreement considered in the economic context in which it is to be applied.

220. Based on the above, it follows from the proposition that subjective intention is not a necessary condition to characterise an agreement as restrictive by object that the courts have held that it is irrelevant that the agreement was not in the commercial interest of some of the participants, and that, where an agreement has an anticompetitive object, it does not cease to be characterised as such because it had an alternative, lawful purpose.

41. Appeal No. 2017/CCPT/001/CON.

221. Furthermore, the fact that it does not need to demonstrate, for example, that horizontal price-fixing agreements produce adverse economic effects relieves it of some of the burden that would otherwise rest upon it. In *T-Mobile*, the court provided that the classification of certain types of agreement as restrictive by object sensibly conserves resources of competition authorities and the justice system.

222. The court above emphasised that the concept of restriction by object should not be given an unduly broad interpretation, nor should it be interpreted so narrowly as to deprive it of its practical effectiveness.

223. The Zambian Competition and Consumer Protection Board in the case of the *Insurers Association of Zambia and 15 Others v. The Competition and Consumer Protection Commission* case endorsed the view that agreements 'containing obvious restrictions of competition such as price-fixing, market-sharing or the control of outlets' – without using the terminology referred to objects but the court considered that agreements of this nature should be deemed to be having the object of restricting competition.

224. Where the parties to an agreement, decision or concerted practice that is restrictive by object wish to assert that it could produce efficiency-enhancing effects, they can do so only by proving that it satisfies the criteria of sections 18 to 21 of the Act which deal with legal exceptions to the rule against restrictive agreements, the burden of proof being on them to prove that this is so.

225. Lastly, the fact that there is no need to prove anticompetitive effects in the case of object restrictions does not mean that there is no quantitative component to object analysis at all. There is a rule that any restriction of competition must be appreciable: even a restriction of competition by object could fall outside section 8 of the Competition and Consumer Protection Act if it's likely impact on the market is minimal.

226. An agreement only infringes section 8 of the Act only if it has an appreciable effect on trade in Zambia. The notion of restriction of competition by object cannot be reduced to an exhaustive list, and that it should not be limited just to the examples of anticompetitive agreements given in sections 9 and 10 of the Competition and Consumer Protection Act.

III. Merger Tests

227. A merger transaction requires authorisation by the Commission where the combined turnover or assets, whichever is higher, in Zambia of the merging parties is at least 50 million fee units in the merging parties' most recent financial year in which these figures are available. Fifty million fee units is equivalent to ZMW 15 million. There are circumstances, however, in which transactions falling below the above thresholds may be investigated. The Commission may, where it has reasonable grounds to believe that a merger falls below the prescribed thresholds, review the merger if the following factors exist:

- the merger is likely to create a position of dominance in a localised product or geographical market;
- the merger is likely to contribute to the creation of a dominant position through a series of acquisitions that are not individually subject to prior notification;
- the merger may substantially prevent or lessen competition;
- the merger is concluded outside Zambia and has consequences in Zambia that require further consideration; or
- as a result of the merger there are, or are likely to be, competition and public interest factors that must be considered.

Chapter 4. Overview of Main Notions

§1. Undertaking

228. Section 3 of the Competition and Consumer Protection Act defines an undertaking as a commitment, promise or other future conduct that a person or enterprise provides to the Commission in order to address any concern raised by the Commission.

229. The definition of undertaking above is not relevant here because as it relates in competition law, what is referred to as undertaking internationally is referred to as an enterprise in the Zambian Competition and Consumer Protection Act. The Act in section 3 defines an enterprise as a firm, partnership, joint venture, corporation, company, association and other juridical persons, which engage in commercial activities, and includes their branches, subsidiaries, affiliates or other entities, directly or indirectly, controlled by them.

230. The term 'enterprise' is critical because only agreements, decisions or concerted practices between enterprises are subject to sections 8, 9, 10 and 12 of the Competition and Consumer Protection Act in relation to restrictive agreement and similarly sections 15 and 16 of the Act referring to dominance and abuse only applies only to abuses committed by dominant enterprises. It should be noted that section 8 of the Competition and Consumer Protection Act also applies to decisions by associations of trade associations.

§2. Relevant Market

231. The Competition and Consumer Protection Act defines a market as in relation to any goods or services, includes a market for those goods or services and other goods or services that are substitutable for, or otherwise competitive with, the goods or services.

232. The Minister may, on the advice of the Commission, prescribe the procedure for determining the relevant product market within which the share of supply or acquisition thresholds are to be met. To date, this procedure has not been outlined by the Minister.

§3. Market Power/Dominant Position

233. Abusive behaviour by a firm that has a dominant position on the market is unlawful. For this purpose a firm is dominant when it has substantial market power that enables it to behave independently on the market without regard to competitors, customers and ultimately consumers. Abuses may be 'exclusionary' or 'exploitative'; in some cases an abuse may be harmful to the single market.

234. An example of an exclusionary abuse would be where a dominant firm reduces its prices to less than cost in order to drive a competitor out of the market or to deter a competitor from entering it, a phenomenon known as predatory pricing. An example of an exploitative abuse would be for the dominant firm to charge an excessive price for its products.

235. As discussed above, section 16 of the Consumer Protection Act provides that an enterprise shall refrain from any act or conduct if, through abuse or acquisition of a dominant position of market power, the act or conduct limits access to markets or otherwise unduly restrains competition, or has or is likely to have adverse effect on trade or the economy in general.

236. The main purpose of this provision is to maximise long-term social welfare through effective competition, competitive harm can thus be defined as a restriction of competition or an exploitation of the dominant position that harms social welfare in the long term.

237. The Competition and Consumer Protection Act defines a dominant position as a situation where an enterprise or a group of enterprises possesses such economic strength in a market as to make it possible for it to operate in that. market, and to adjust prices or output, without effective constraint from competitors or potential competitors.

238. Dominance can therefore be equated to the concept of substantial market power that is used in economics. The notion of independence is related to the degree of competitive constraint exerted on the undertaking under investigation.

239. Therefore, where competitive constraints are ineffective, the undertaking in question enjoys substantial market power over a period of time, an undertaking has substantial market power if it is capable of profitably increasing prices above the competitive level for a significant period of time. As will be seen below, abusing this dominant position is not permitted under Zambian competition law.

§4. Agreements, Decisions and Concerted Practices

240. It is important to highlight that in terms of section 8 of the Competition and Consumer Protection Act, conduct which amounts to an agreement, decision or concerted practice is outlawed. It is therefore imperative to give meaning to what 'agreement, decision or concerted practice' means.

241. As section 8 is not limited to legal contracts but also applied to cooperation achieved through informal agreements, decisions or concerted practices, we need to examine these concepts in detail.

I. Agreements

242. Section 2 of the Competition and Consumer Protection Act defines an agreement as:

> means any form of agreement, whether or not legally enforceable, between enterprises which is implemented or intended to be implemented in Zambia and includes an oral agreement or a decision by a trade association or an association of enterprises;

243. The word 'agreement' in Zambian competition law centres around the existence of a concurrence of wills between at least two parties, the form in which it is manifested being unimportant so long as it constitutes the faithful expression of the parties' intention.

244. For an agreement to be deemed to be anticompetitive, there must be a 'concurrence of wills' must be to limit competition in the market. Further, that concurrence of wills must manifest itself into 'a faithful expression of the parties' intention'. The Tribunal in *the Insurers Association of Zambia v. The Competition and Consumer Protection Commission* confirmed that establishing the faithful expression of the parties' intention by the concurrence of the wills is subjective. The Tribunal did state that determining subjective intention can only be determined by the conduct of the persons concerned.

245. There is a reason why the case law emphasised the need for a concurrence of wills which has the intention of limiting competition. The reason is that associations or members of single industries often meet to discuss various issues and make agreements in line with their meetings and discussions. To hold that every meeting held amounts to anticompetitive behaviour would be absurd. It therefore follows that the concurrence of wills must be to limit competition. This would mean that associations would never meet to discuss matters of common interest.

246. As highlighted above, in determining the object of an agreement, regard must be had to the content of its provisions, the objectives it seeks to ascertain and the economic and legal context which it forms part.

247. Determining the anticompetitive behaviour cannot be achieved based simply on a meeting and the content of the resolution – wider considerations need to be considered. With regard to the objective the meeting sought to ascertain, the intention of the parties should be taken into account (objective) or whether or not the effect would have been to restrict competition.

248. A legal contract, without doubt qualifies as an agreement that would be covered by the Act. This would include a compromise of litigation such as a trademark delimitation agreement or the settlement of a breach of patent action in the courts of Zambia. Further, informal agreements such as simple understandings and gentleman's agreements have also been accepted as agreements even though they are not strictly legally binding as there isn't a requirement that an agreement should be supported by enforcement procedures.

249. Any form of agreement which reflects a genuine concurrence of will between parties will constitute an agreement within the meaning of section 8 of the Competition and Consumer Protection Act. These agreements need not be in writing and can be made orally.

250. Furthermore, agreements such as articles of association of companies, constitutions of trade association, exchange of communication such as email correspondence and telephonic conversations and even those agreements which have expired by effluxion of time but effects continue afterwards will be covered by section 8 of the Competition and Consumer Protection Act.

251. Entities cannot justify infringement of the rules in the Competition and Consumer Protection Act by producing a defence that they were forced into an agreement by the conduct of other companies or their competitors. However, where an entity entered into an agreement unwillingly, the Competition and Consumer Protection Commission may mitigate the fine or should not impose any penalty at all.

252. The fact that natural person who entered into the agreement did not have authority to enter into a restrictive agreement does not mean that the undertaking that employs them is not liable. Under Section 23(1)*(b)*(iii) of the Companies Act, a company is still bound even if the company's director or officer was not authorised to exercise powers.

253. In *Finance Bank Zambia Limited and 4 Others v. Zambezi Portland Cement Limited,*[42] a dispute arose where the persons claiming to be shareholders of Zambezi Portland commenced court proceedings against Leasing Finance Company Limited to claim damages for unlawful retention of money and loss of business. The other party claiming ownership in Zambezi Portland sued claiming that those persons lacked the authority to commence court process as they were not even the correct shareholders.

254. In a judgment delivered by Wood JS, the Zambia Supreme Court held by virtue of the law (based on provisions of the old Companies Act which are similar to the current Act), even though court process was commenced without authority, no acts of a company are invalidated on the grounds that the acts were contrary to the articles of association or the director/agent lacked authority.

255. Further, where a formal agreement is reached but there isn't agreement on all matters between the parties, the aspects of the agreement that are restrictive in nature will be subject to liability under the Competition and Consumer Protection Act.

---

42. SCZ Appeal No. 144/2015.

256. Many cartels which constitute agreements to price fix or limit supply of goods or services are not always simple. In some cases, not always, members of a cartel actually meet and behave precisely in concert with one another. This is the most patent way cartel agreements appear in Zambia but to avoid being obvious about their conduct, this is rarely the case and not always have cartels operate.

257. In most cases, they are complex and ensure for a long period of time. Over a period of time, some entities may be more active than others in the running of a cartel, whilst some entities may renege or drop out for a short period of time but subsequently re-enter – and in some cases, others may attend meetings or communicate in other ways in order to be kept informed, without necessarily intending to fall in line with the agreed plan.

258. In the instances described above where the nature of the cartel agreement is not so clear, the Competition and Consumer Protection Commission would have difficulty in proving discrete agreements to deduce if they fall foul of the Competition and Consumer Protection Act.

259. Sections 8 and 9 of the Competition and Consumer Protection Act envisages the concept of a single, overall agreement to deduce whether an agreement meets the requirements of competition law. To hold companies and entities accountable for any breach. Where there is a consensus between parties such that it forms a single, overall agreement, such agreement will be binding even if it was oral, not strictly legally binding and no sanctions for its enforcement.

260. It follows that in seeking to deduce whether there was an agreement in terms of section 8 of the Competition and Consumer Protection Act, an entity will be liable, where there is evidence that they participated in one or some of the elements of the agreements.

II. Decisions

261. Coordination between independent undertakings may be achieved through organisations that operate in a specific industry. Example of such organisations are the Millers Association of Zambia, Insurers Association of Zambia, Law Association of Zambia or the Zambia National Farmers Union to mention but a few.

262. Where these type of organisations take decisions that are anticompetitive, they will be subject to section 8 of the Competition and Consumer Protection Act. The organisation itself and its members may all be fined by the Competition and Consumer Protection Commission where they make decisions that seek to restrict competition.

263. Based on the above, even the founding document, regulations or constitution of an organisation would constitute both an agreement and a decision for the purposes of section 8 of the Competition and Consumer Protection Act.

264. Even recommendations made by the organisation to its members also constitute a decision even if it is not a binding recommendation and was not unanimously accepted by all members of the organisation.

265. In the case of the *Insurers Association of Zambia and 15 Others v. The Competition and Consumer Protection Commission*, the Competition and Consumer Protection Board provided that even though a recommendation was not binding, its effect could restrict competition if implemented and the parties were thus liable. In this case an organisation made up of water-supply entities recommended to its members not to connect dishwashing machines to a system which did not have a label supplied by a Belgian association of producers. It was held that this was anti-competitive as it would have the effect of discriminating against other appliances produced in other countries.

266. Specifically, with recommendations, it would be prudent for the Competition and Consumer Protection Commission to investigate and consider whether the members of an organisation have in the past tended to comply with the recommendation and whether compliance with such recommendation would have a significant influence on competition within the relevant market.

267. Section 8 of the Competition and Consumer Protection Act does not only apply to agreements and concerted practices between undertaking, but also applies to decisions of associations of undertaking or organisations that encompass several enterprises. For example, a decision by a group of milling companies under the Millers Association of Zambia to fix prices for mealie meal could be deemed to be unfair competition under this provision.

268. Further, such an association need not have its own economic or commercial activity to be subject to the provision, all that is required to be proven is that they acted in a manner contrary to section 9 of the Competition and Consumer Protection Act.

269. It therefore follows that section 8 of the Competition and Consumer Protection Act may apply to the decisions of association, even if it does not apply to its agreements because the association/ group does not enter into the agreements as an undertaking. Where the association is an undertaking, an agreement between it and other undertaking would be covered by the provision as well.

270. However as noted earlier, statutory monopolies are exempt from the provisions of the Act and those relating to restrictive agreements provided that they that do not enter into an agreement that has the purpose of restricting competition; or whose conduct does not, in itself or in conjunction with another enterprise, amount to an abuse of a dominant position; or that wishes to enter into a merger transaction, is in compliance with. the provisions of this Act relating to mergers. Further, certain sectors are also exempt from the Act namely the pension, energy, communications and Bank of Zambia sector.

271. Further, even if the decision to limit competition is subsequently approved and extended in scope by a government or public agency does not mean that the agreements falls outside the scope of the Act. It therefore follows that even if an association has statutory functions or has members approved by the government, any horizontal agreements are not exempt from being considered anticompetitive behaviour. However, please note that if there is a statutory monopoly or a particular sector that is protected, then this principle does not apply as these are exempt from application of the Act provided the criteria is met. This will be discussed further below.

III. Concerted Practices

272. Conduct which is not attributable to an agreement or a decision may nevertheless amount to an infringement of section 8 of the Competition and Consumer Protection Act. Section 3 of the Competition and Consumer Protection Act defines a concerted practice as:

> a practice which involves some form of communication or coordination between competitors falling short of an actual agreement but which replaces their independent action and restricts or lessens competition between them;

273. The above definition emphasises that conduct will be anticompetitive if it amounts to any form of communication or coordination that restricts competition. The rationale for the inclusion of concerted practices is that in some cases, entities or organisations or associations might try to conceal agreements or decisions or any other form of coordinated effort to act in an anticompetitive manner. Entities should thus not escape liability if they act in a manner that is anticompetitive. Just because there is no evidence or lack of a firm agreement or decision.

274. To this end, it is necessary to also include the manner in which companies act within the ambit of competition law to appropriately deduce if their conduct is anticompetitive notwithstanding the lack of a decision or agreement.

275. A concerted practice is established where there is a form of coordination between undertakings which, without having reached the stage where an agreement properly so-called has been concluded, knowingly substitutes practical cooperation between them for the risks of competition.

276. For a concerted practice, there is no need to prove an actual plan to restrict competition. What is required to be shown is any direct or indirect contact between such operators, the object or effect whereof is either to influence the conduct on the market of an actual or potential competitor or to disclose to such a competitor the course of conduct which they themselves have decided to adopt or contemplate adopting on the market.

277. Therefore, for a concerted practice to exist, there must be a mental consensus whereby practical cooperation is knowingly substituted for competition; however, the consensus need not be achieved verbally, and can come about by direct or indirect contact between the parties.

278. The question that arises is whether or not a concerted practice needs to have been put into effect for it to be caught by section 8 of the Competition and Consumer Protection Act. Even in the absence of anticompetitive effect on the market, a concerted practice can be established and be subject to competition law. This accords with section 8 of the Competition and Consumer Protection Act which provides that the concerted practice must have the object of restricting or distorting competition.

279. There is a presumption of a causal connection between the contact of a competitor and conduct in deducting whether a concerted practice is liable. Thus, where there is a casual connection between the conduct of the market and how competitors act then the concerted practice will be subject to liability under section 8 of the Competition and Consumer protection Act.

280. The Zambian decisions have not gone further to provide that the concept of concerted practice implies that there will be common conduct on the market due to the concerted practice and if there is a causal connection between the practice and market conduct then the practice will be contrary to competition law. This accords with section 8 of the Competition and Consumer Protection Act which provides that the concerted practice must have the effect of restricting or distorting competition.

281. A concerted practice exists if its object or effect is to distort or restrict competition as is provided in Zambia's Competition and Consumer Protection Act. Thus, in theory if the concerted practice does not have an effect on the market, but its object was to restrict competition then it would be subject to section 8.

282. The burden of proof lies on the Competition and Consumer Protection Commission to establish that there has been a concerted practice. However, if there is clear evidence that there is a casual connection between the contact of a competitor and the conduct of the market, then the burden will be on the applicable company or organisation to disprove a concerted practice.

§5. Restriction of Competition

283. The Competition and Consumer Protection Act is responsible for restrictions and distortions of competition, for example, as a result of legislative measures, regulations, licensing rules or the provision of subsidies. Some systems of competition law give a role to competition authorities to scrutinise 'public' restrictions of competition and to play a 'competition advocacy' role by commenting on, and even recommending the removal of, such restrictions.

284. Section 8 of the Competition and Consumer Protection Act which states that any category of agreement, decision or concerted practice which its object or effect has as, the prevention, restriction or distortion of competition to an appreciable extent in Zambia is anticompetitive are prohibited.

285. What is clear from the above is that the Competition Act prohibits any agreement or decisions that have the 'object' or 'effect' of preventing, restricting or distorting competition. The definition of agreement in the Act encompasses any decision that has either been implemented or intended to be implemented.

286. The key words in Section 8 are therefore 'object' or 'effect'. What is clear from the provision in the Competition and Consumer Protection Act is there the words 'object or effect' have to be read disjunctively. It is clear that these are alternative, and neither cumulative nor simultaneous requirement for a finding of the infringement of section 8 of the Competition and Consumer Protection Act.

287. In other words, where an agreement has as its object the restriction of competition, it is unnecessary to provide if it has anticompetitive effects as well – only one, either the object or effect has to be proven.

288. What is clear from the provisions in the Act read together with the applicable case law is that section 8 of the Competition and Consumer Protection Act prohibits certain agreements that have the object of restricting competition, irrespective of whether they produce adverse effects on the market, and the same is true vice-versa - the Act prohibits agreements that have the effect of restricting competition, irrespective of whether they had an adverse object to restrict competition.

289. Only when it is not clear that the object of the agreement is to restrict competition will it be necessary to consider the effect of the restrictive agreement. The meaning of object or effect will be considered under the balancing test under tests for illegality, balancing tests.

I. Horizontal Agreements

290. Section 9(1) of the Competition Act provides that:-

(1) A horizontal agreement between enterprises is prohibited per se, and void, if the agreement:
   (a) fixes, directly or indirectly, a purchase or selling price or any other trading conditions;
   (b) divides markets by allocating customers, suppliers or territories specific types of goods or services;
   (c) involves bid rigging, unless the person requesting the bid is informed of the terms of the agreement prior to the making of the bid;
   (d) sets production quotas; or
   (e) provides for collective refusal to deal in, or supply, goods or services.

291. A horizontal agreement relates to an agreement, decision or concerted practice between competitors.

292. Horizontal agreements that involve the hardcore cartel activities of price-fixing, market-sharing, and bid rigging, as well as production limitation agreements, and boycotts and joint refusals to deal are per se prohibited. Stiff penalties for entering into per se prohibited horizontal agreements are provided for in line with the seriousness of the offence. Fines of up to 10% of annual turnover can be imposed on enterprises.

293. The Competition and Consumer Protection Tribunal in the case of *Top Gear and Nine Others v. Competition and Consumer Protection Commission,*[43] dealt with several garages that engaged in a cartel to deliberately fix trading conditions in the market. The garages in that case were charging customers for obtaining quotation for the repair of motor vehicles.

294. The Competition and Consumer Protection Tribunal in the *Top Gear* case stated that a horizontal agreement is not permitted where it clearly intends to fix either directly or indirectly, a purchase or selling price or any other trading conditions. According to the Tribunal in that case, the documentation must be clear to satisfy the Tribunal that the conduct contravened section 9(1) of the Competition Act.

II. Vertical Agreements

295. Section 10 (1) and (2) of the Competition and Consumer Protection Act provides as follows:

(1) A vertical agreement between enterprises is prohibited per se, and void, to the extent that it involves resale price maintenance.
(2) Notwithstanding subsection (1), a supplier or producer may recommend a minimum resale price to the reseller of a good or a service if:
    (a) the supplier or producer makes it clear to the reseller that the recommendation is not binding; and
    (b) the product has a price stated on it and the words "recommended price" appear next to the stated price.

296. Unlike horizontal agreements, vertical agreements do not involve a combination of market power but rather involve agreements between suppliers and buyers or other entities at different levels of the distribution supply chain to act in an anticompetitive manner.

297. The best way to describe vertical agreements is through the illustration of a distribution chain A supplier of services or producer of goods will either require

43. 2012/CPT/003.

them for their own consumption and use or will want to supply them to the market. An enterprise seeking to sell their services or products to the market must decide how to do so. This can be done and carried out both by the production and the sales and distribution functions itself – which is vertical integration. Such integration may use the services of an agent to assist the supplier to find customers, but as is often the case in Zambia, supply of the products to an independent distributor whose role is to resell the products to other people or companies.

298. Under these arrangements, different levels on the supply chain could choose to enter agreements to subvert fair competition such as promoting the products in exchange for lower prices.

III. Single Economic Unit

299. Section 13 of the Competition and Consumer Protection Act provides that the provisions related to horizontal and vertical agreements do not apply to an agreement to which all the parties involved are interconnected bodies corporate falling under a single economic unit.

300. Therefore, where two or more legal persons form a single economic entity: collectively comprising a single undertaking, any agreements between two or more of these entities will not fall within the scope of the Competition and Consumer Protection Act. An example of such an agreement would be one between a subsidiary company and its parent company or between a contractor and a subcontractor.

301. Firms within the same corporate group can enter into legally enforceable agreements with one another but such agreement will not fall within section 9 or 10 of the Competition and Consumer Protection Act. Here it must be shown that the relationship between them is so close that economically they form a single economic entity, i.e., that they consist of a unitary organisation of personal, tangible and intangible elements, which pursue a specific economic aim on a long-term basis and can contribute to the commission of an infringement of the kind referred to sections 9, 10 and 12 of the Competition and Consumer Protection Act. In such an instance, the agreement is regarded as the internal allocation of functions within the economic group rather than a horizontal or vertical agreement between independent undertakings.

302. The reasoning above undoubtedly also applies where a company or enterprise exercises decisive influence over another company as they would essentially form a single economic unit as they are part of the same undertaking. The same also applies to sister companies where companies over which decisive influence is exercised by the same parent company occurs. In such cases, as will be explored later, if the two or more companies merge, they need to comply with the provisions of the Competition and Consumer Protection Act by meeting the criteria and getting the necessary approval.

303. It therefore follows that a critical question needs to be deduced – how control is determined. In other words, one needs to determine whether the parties to an agreement are independent in how they exercise their decision-making or whether one is able to exercise decisive influence over the other, with the result being that the second company does not actually enjoy real autonomy in determining its economic or commercial functions.

304. The factors that are relevant when determining control of by a parent company are the composition of the board of directors in all entities involved, the shareholding that the parent company has over its subsidiary and the extent to which the parent company influences the policy or commercial direction or issues instructions to the subsidiary and similar matters.

305. In *Imperial Chemical Industries v. Commission*,[44] the court held that where a parent company has 100% shareholding in a subsidiary, there is a rebuttable presumption that the parent company exercises decisive influence over that subsidiary. The court thereby held that they operated as an economic unit and not subject to the provisions on restrictive agreements.

306. However, what is not completely clear is whether a minority shareholder might be held to have sufficient control to negate the autonomy on the part of a subsidiary as the *Imperial Chemicals* case provided that this only applies where a parent company owns the totality or almost all of the subsidiary company or controls a majority of its affairs.

307. There are some cases where the single economic entity doctrine will not apply. In the seminar *Ijsselcentrale*[45] case, four different electricity companies claimed they were in a joint venture that formed a single economic unit. The Commission in that case rejected that argument because they did not form one unit but rather were separate legal entities that were not controlled by a single nature or legal person.

308. Thus, even though the companies formed part of an indivisible system of public electricity supply, the fact that they were able to determine their own conduct independently and were not subject to control from a single or the same unit meant that they could not be considered as a single economic unit. This case demonstrates with clarity where the single economic unit argument would not work under section 13 of the Zambian Competition and Consumer Protection Act.

309. Further, where a subsidiary company becomes independent from its parent company, such as when the subsidiary is bought by another entity, any agreement between the two could be caught by section 8 of the Competition and Consumer

44. (1972) CMLR 557.
45. (1992) 5 CMLR 154.

Protection Act. This is because the subsidiary-parent company relationship has ended and thus they are no longer a single economic unit that is protected under the law.

310. As can be seen from the above, there are various consequences that result from the single economic unit doctrine under the Competition and Consumer Protection Act. First, although an agreement between connected companies may not infringe section 8 of the Act, the manipulation of a subsidiary company by a parent company might mean that the rules of competition law in Zambia are broken in other ways such as a parent company ordering its subsidiaries to impose production quotas or export banks. Such an agreement would infringe the provisions of the Act.

311. Therefore, whereas the single economic unit is a doctrine recognised by the Competition Act, there are circumstances where agreements could fall foul of sections 8, 9, 10 or 12 of the Act where, for example, the parent company ordered a subsidiary to enter into a cartel or some other agreement beyond the scope of an internal arrangement between the companies.

312. In the circumstances where a subsidiary is liable for infringing an aspect of the Competition and Consumer Protection Act, the Court of Justice in *Akzo Nobel NV v Commission*[46] held that the parent company that controls the subsidiary could be liable jointly and severally for any fine imposed on the subsidiary unless the parent company can adduce sufficient evidence that the subsidiary acts independently.

A. Separate Legal Personality and Corporate Reorganisation

313. A company is in law regarded as a legal entity separate and distinct from the members who make it up. As an artificial legal person, a company will be entitled to deal with other persons, natural or artificial, in its own name and in its own right. Section 16 of the Companies Act provides that

> a company registered in accordance with the Companies Act, acquires a separate legal status, with the name by which it is registered, and shall continue to exist as a corporate until it is removed from the Register of Companies.

314. This provision codifies a principle from the common law that the owners of the business (shareholders) are separate from the company itself.

315. Further, by section 22(b) of the Companies Act 'a company shall have, subject to this Act and to such limitations as are inherent in its corporate nature, the capacity rights, powers and privileges of an individual.'

316. In the post privatisation era, the Zambian Supreme Court has had occasion to consider the concept of corporate personality on numerous occasions. The court

46. (2009) 5 CMLR 2633.

was, not unexpectedly, called upon in many cases before it to consider the question whether the change in the ownership of the shares in various previously state-owned companies amounted to a change in the companies themselves. In *Kankomba and Others v. Chilanga Cement Plc,*[47] for instance, the appellants were employed by Chilanga Cement Ltd which was a wholly Government of Zambia owned company under ZIMCO (Zambia Industrial & Mining Company). In 1994, Chilanga Cement Limited was taken over by the Commonwealth Development Corporation (CDC). To be precise, the shares of Chilanga Cement Limited were bought by CDC and the company became a public company hence its title changed to Chilanga Cement Plc (Public Limited Company). This means that Chilanga Cement Company Limited was no longer a private company, but a public company.

317. The line of business remains the same and the employees who included the appellants were the same. In due course, the new owners of the company changed management. In April 1995, the new management introduced new conditions of service which the appellants, in some cases, alleged were inferior to the previous conditions. They were particularly concerned that some allowances which were previously paid separately and in conformity with the Statutory Instrument No. 99 were then fused into their salaries. Such allowances included lunch, and funeral grant. Also under the new conditions, the early retirement service period was increased from ten years of service to twenty years of service, contrary to what the statutory instrument provided (at ten years).

318. The appellants felt that, in view of these changes, their conditions of service were changed to their detriment and that they should have been given an option to retire as from 31st March 1995, on old ZIMCO conditions and re-engaged under the new conditions for those who want to continue working for the company and when they retired under the new conditions of service, be paid gratuity under the new terms.

319. The defence contended that there was no change of employer as what was involved was a mere change of shareholding and the company continued operating as a going concern. The employees were informed of the changes. The employees were free to resign and, in this spirit, the General Manager resigned. It was denied that the new conditions of service were discriminatory or inferior. On the contrary it was argued that they were superior. The funeral grant was increased from ZMW 30,000.00 to ZMW 50,000.00. In addition, coffin, transport, firewood and money incidental to the funeral were to be given under the revised conditions. Further, under the new conditions of service, under redundancy the employee is to be given six months' notice as against one month under Statutory Instrument No. 99 of 1994, and three and a half months' pay as against three months' basic pay under the Statutory Instrument.

320. On the evidence and the long submissions before him, the learned trial judge found that most of what was pleaded was not supported by any evidence. He

47. SCZ Judgment No. 30 of 2002.

found as a fact that there was no change of employer so as to call upon the appellants and others to exercise their option of continuing to serve with the new employees; he found that the new conditions of service were not discriminatory and disadvantageous to the appellants; instead they were superior conditions of service. He found that there was no need to request the appellant to exercise the option of whether to retire or continue serving under the new shareholders and management and that Section 35 of the Employment Act did not apply to the appellants. He therefore dismissed the appellant's claims with costs. The Supreme Court agreed that a change in the shareholders did not mean a change of the company.

321. On identical facts the court came to the same conclusion in *ZCCM and Ndola Lime Company Limited v. Sikanyika and Others*[48] where it cited with approval the case of *Salomon v. Salomon.* It held once again that the change of ownership of shares in a company does not result in the corporate entity becoming a new employer. The court recognised the distinction between the company as a body corporate and the shareholders in that company.

322. The *Newton Siulanda and Others v. Foodcorp Products Ltd*[49] case brought up substantively nothing new. The workers sought a declaration that there had been a change of employer without their consent when all the shares in Zamhort Products (Zambia) Limited were bought by Foodcorp Products Limited or when the name was changed from the former to latter. The appellant workers contented that there had been disadvantageous unilateral alteration of their conditions of service when a 'new' employer was introduced and accordingly that there was a breach by the employer of their contracts of employment entitling the workers to treat the contract as repudiated. The Supreme Court per Ngulube CJ, as he then was, in dismissing the appeal stated *inter alia* that:

323. The principle of separate legal personality is critical in the context of competition law in Zambia, especially as it relates to corporate reorganisation. Separate legal entities may be treated as one and the same undertaking where there is a corporate reorganisation in which one entity succeeds another. In such circumstances, the liabilities of the latter company may be attributed to the former company.

324. An important question arises where one entity commits an infringement of the rules in the Competition and Consumer Protection Act, but then sells the business that was responsible for the infringement to a third party.

325. It is obvious that in such circumstances, the purchaser will need to know whether it bears the risk of a future fine in the event of the Competition and Consumer Protection Commission adopting a decision. It is also clear that, the basic rule of personal responsibility is that, if the undertaking that was responsible for the business is still in existence, it remains liable for the infringement rather than the

48. SCZ Judgment No. 24 of 2002.
49. [2000] ZR 36.

company that acquired it. In *BASF v. Commission*,[50] the court concluded that where a company commits an infringement of competition law and withdraws from the market or sells part of the business responsible, it will still be held liable if it is still in existence.

326. However, the new company that purchased the business will be liable if the former corporate entity which committed the violation ceases to exist in law after the infringement was committed.

B. Piercing the Corporate Veil for Abuse: Single Economic Entity

327. The concepts of separate legal personality of company and limited liability operate as a shield to holding shareholders directly and personally liable for debts of the company. The wall or curtain separating the company from its individual shareholders and directors is commonly referred to as 'veil of incorporation'.

328. However, the veil of incorporation is not an unassailable right or privilege. As Malila JS of the Zambian Supreme Court stated in the case of *Madison Investment, Property and Advisory Company Limited v. Peter Kanyinji*:[51]

> Notwithstanding the significance of observing the distinction between the corporation and its owners, courts ought to be careful to ensure that there is some limit to the protection given by the notion of separate corporate personality so that business dealings remain honest.

329. Therefore, although a company is in law regarded as a separate and distinct entity from the members comprising it, there are instances when it is justified to abandon the notion of corporate personality and to peer behind the façade of separate legal personality to see the human persons behind the legal persona for the purpose of holding them accountable for the actions of the company. This is called lifting or piercing the corporate veil.

330. Therefore, just because companies will not be subject to the provisions of the Competition Act where they operate as a single economic unit, they could still be liable and liability could attract to those controlling the company.

331. It should be noted that the terms 'lifting the veil' and 'piercing the veil' are used interchangeably. Some have interpreted the two terms to have separate meanings. Lifting has been associated with merely looking behind the corporate veil to see who the true owners or controllers of the company are whilst piercing the veil

50. (1995) ECR II-729.
51. Selected Judgment No. 48 of 2018.

has been interpreted as attaching personal liability to the controllers in given circumstances. The one more relevant to Competition Law is lifting the corporate view where a company is operating as a single unit or being used for some fraudulent purpose.

332. It is submitted that the two terms are essentially the same in Zambia because there is a requirement for every company to maintain a register of beneficial owners,[52] so a court will always be aware of who the true controllers are. Therefore, both terms are used to show that the court will look behind the veil and attach liability.

333. The concept of piercing the corporate veil was stated as follows by the Supreme Court per Silomba JS in *Swallow Freight Services (Zambia) Limited v. Kapili Transport Company Limited*:[53]

> It is our law, both under the common law and under our statute, that once a company is incorporated it becomes a legal entity or person with its own identity separate from those who own or direct it, (per *Salomon v. Salomon and Company*). However, as the above quote strongly suggests, the company's corporate veil, that imaginary legal 'curtain' that separates the company from its shareholders or those who direct and control it, can be pierced in circumstances where: (I) the court wants to do justice in a matter before it; (ii) by treating the company as identical with the person or persons who control it. The piercing of the corporate veil will be ordered not only where there is fraud or improper conduct but where the character of the company or those who control it, is relevant to the proceedings.

334. Therefore, the courts will not normally look beyond the facades of the company to the shareholders who comprise it but only where there is proof that the entity is concealing or evading its obligations to another, fraudulently.

§6. Monopolisation and Abuse of Dominance

335. There are several reasons against monopolisation and why the Competition and Consumer Protection Act seeks to guard against monopolies. The monopolist is in a position to affect the market price. This is because it is responsible for all the output, and since aggregate output determines price through the relationship of supply to demand, the monopolist will be able either to increase price by reducing the volume of its own production or to reduce sales by increasing price: the latter occurs in the case of highly branded products which are sold at a high price, such as luxury perfumes.

52. Section 195 of the Companies Act.
53. SCZ Appeal No. 81 of 2006.

336. It should be noted that under section 3(e) of the Competition and Consumer Protection Act, business of any enterprise exercising a statutory monopoly which precludes the entry of another enterprise into the relevant market in Zambia are excluded from the application of the Act due largely to then nature of the public benefit the service and goods they provide are.

337. These businesses that operate as statutory monopolies are only protected if the enterprise does not enter into an agreement that has the purpose of restricting competition; the conduct of the enterprise does not, in itself or in conjunction with another enterprise, amount to an abuse of a dominant position; or the enterprise, if it wishes to enter into a merger transaction, is in compliance with the provisions of this Act relating to mergers.

338. However, Zambia monopolies that maximise profits see that it will be able to earn the largest profit if it refrains from expanding its production to the level that would be attained under perfect competition. The result will be that output is lower than would be the case under perfect competition and that therefore some consumers will be deprived of goods and services that they would have been prepared to pay for at the competitive market price. There is therefore allocative inefficiency in this situation: society's resources are not distributed in the most efficient way possible. The extent of this allocative inefficiency is sometimes referred to as the 'deadweight loss' attributable to monopoly; this is a pure loss to society, rather than simply a transfer of resources from consumers to the monopolist.

339. There is also the problem that productive efficiency may be lower because the monopolist is not constrained by competitive forces to reduce costs to the lowest possible level. Instead the firm becomes 'X-inefficient'. This term, first used by Liebenstein, refers to a situation in which resources are used to make the right product, but less productively than they might be: management spends too much time on the golf course, outdated industrial processes are maintained and a general slackness pervades the organisation of the firm.

340. Furthermore, the monopolist may not feel the need to innovate, because it does not experience the constant pressure to go on attracting custom by offering better, more advanced, products. Thus, it has been said that the greatest benefit of being a monopolist is the quiet life it is able to enjoy. However, it is important to bear in mind that inefficient managers of a business may be affected by pressures other than those of competition. In particular their position may be undermined by uninvited takeover bids on stock exchanges from investors who consider that more efficient use could be made of the firm's assets. Competition may be felt in capital as well as product markets: this is sometimes referred to as 'the market for corporate control'.

341. Since it can charge a higher price than in conditions of competition (it is a price-maker), wealth is transferred from the unfortunate consumer to the monopolist. Some economists would argue that this point is irrelevant: social welfare is concerned with allocative and productive efficiency; and for these purposes it is irrelevant whether wealth lies in the monopolist's or the consumer's hands. While it is not the function of competition authorities themselves to determine how society's wealth should be distributed, it is manifestly a legitimate matter for Governments to take an interest in economic equity, and it may be that one of the ways in which policy is expressed on this issue is through competition law21.

342. Abuse of dominant position is prohibited under section 16(1) of the Act. It is not unlawful for a firm to have a dominant position; what is prohibited is the abuse of a dominant position. However, the Court of Justice in *Michelin v. Commission*,[54] stated that a firm in a dominant position has a 'special responsibility not to allow its conduct to impair undistorted competition' on the internal market.

343. It is clear that section 16 of the Competition and Consumer Protection Act imposes obligations on dominant firms that non-dominant firms do not bear. Unilateral behaviour is not controlled under section 8 of the Competition and Consumer Protection Act, which applies only to collusive conduct; unilateral acts however can amount to an infringement of section 16 of the Competition and Consumer Protection Act.

344. Section 16 of the Competition and Consumer Protection Act gives examples of conduct that is abusive – charging unfair prices, limiting production and discrimination that places certain trading parties at a competitive disadvantage – but this list is not exhaustive.

345. A difficulty with section 16 of the Competition and Consumer Protection Act is that the line between pro-competitive and anticompetitive conduct is not always an easy one to draw, and there is an obvious danger that, if section 16 of the Competition and Consumer Protection Act is applied too aggressively, firms might refrain from conduct that is in fact pro-competitive. Clearly it would be the ultimate paradox if a law designed to promote competition in fact were to have the effect of diminishing it.

346. However, it is equally clear that unduly lenient treatment on the part of competition authorities and courts could lead to the exclusion from the market of efficient competitors, with adverse consequences for the competitive process and consumer welfare.

347. A more stylised way of presenting this problem is to consider the difference between what are sometimes referred to as 'false positives' and 'false negatives:

- A false positive occurs where a competition authority incorrectly concludes that pro-competitive behaviour is abusive: a harm to the firm(s) found guilty, and also to consumers, since the pro-competitive behaviour will be prohibited. The problem here is that the law is overinclusive.

---

54. Case 322/81 EU:C:1983:313.

– A false negative occurs where a competition authority incorrectly concludes that anticompetitive behaviour is not illegal and therefore permits it: a harm to consumers. Here the law is under-inclusive.

348. Given the inherent difficulty of determining which unilateral acts are anticompetitive and which are pro-competitive, it is inevitable that competition authorities will sometimes make errors; a policy question when framing rules on unilateral behaviour is to decide which of the two errors is preferable.

349. Just as it is possible under section 8 of the Competition and Consumer Protection Act for there to be a 'single overall agreement' that violates that provision as discussed, so too it is possible for there to be a 'single overall abuse' (or a 'single and continuous abuse') under section 16 of the Competition and Consumer Protection Act.

350. Section 16 (2) of the Act provides that for purposes of section 16, abuse of a dominant position includes:

– imposing, directly or indirectly, unfair purchase or selling prices or other unfair trading conditions;
– limiting or restricting production, market outlets or market access, investment, technical development or technological progress in a manner that affects competition;
– applying dissimilar conditions to equivalent transactions with other trading parties;
– making the conclusion of contracts subject to acceptance by other parties of supplementary conditions which by their nature or according to commercial usage have no connection with the subject matter of the contracts;
– denying any person access to an essential facility;
– charging an excessive price to the detriment of consumers; or
– selling goods below their marginal or variable cost.

351. The word 'includes' in section 16(2) of the Competition and Consumer Protection Act denotes that these are not an exhaustive list and the Zambian Competition and Consumer Protection Commission can deduce abuse of dominance on situations that are not explicitly outlined.

352. When evaluating whether an entity has abused its dominant position, the court will look carefully at the conduct outlined in section 16(2) of the Competition and Consumer Protection Act and seek to determine whether the conduct of the dominant undertaking prima facie restricts competition or exploits the restriction of competition inherent in the dominant position in a way that runs counter to the purpose of section 16 of the Act as whole. In other words, the test seeks to deduce whether the conduct under review causes competitive harm.

353. It is submitted that section 16(2) of the Competition and Consumer Protection Act merely provides a prima facie case that a dominant undertaking has abused its market power or dominance but it not the complete test as required by established competition law principles.

354. Under the first leg of the test, the competitive harm will be looked at through the lens of the circumstances provided for in the Competition and Consumer Protection Act. Once one of these is established, a prima facie case of competitive harm is caused.

355. However, the second part is also equally important. If a prima facie case of abuse is established, it is always open to the dominant undertaking to adduce sufficient evidence tending to show that its conduct is objectively justified.

356. While the principle of proportionality seeks to balance between prima facie anticompetitive effects and objective justification, it is important to note that the same principle also affects what is a prima facie abuse. This is particularly clear when the case law applies a test of reasonableness or proportionality to determine whether the conduct causes competitive harm.

357. It is therefore submitted based on the above that this is how the abuse of dominant position should be assessed in Zambia rather than merely looking at whether a company with a dominant position committed one of the acts outlawed in section 16(2). The test needs a balancing and proportionality to determine if the conduct is actually anticompetitive and if there may be an objective justification.

358. What is clear from section 16 of the Competition and Consumer Protection Act is that it entails an enquiry as to whether the behaviour of an enterprise based on of the listed grounds in section 16(2) deviates from 'normal' or 'fair' or 'undistorted' competition, or from 'competition on the merits'. It is for this reason that defences and objective justifications are part of the enquiry.

359. Examples of objective justification that could excuse conduct identified in section 16(2) as developed in the *Compagnie Maritime Belge* case are that the conduct under review is a reasonable and proportionate reaction to a commercial threat and, therefore, lawful or it is an abuse of a dominance position and, therefore, prohibited. In *Sot. Lélos*,[55] the court stated that the fact that an undertaking is in a dominant position cannot deprive it of its entitlement to protect its own commercial interests when they are attacked; however, the Court added that such behaviour cannot be allowed if its purpose is to strengthen the dominant position and thereby abuse it. The reasonable and proportionate protection of legitimate commercial interests is not an objective justification because it is inherently incompatible with a prima facie abuse identified in section 16(2) of the Act.

55. C-468/06.

360. The principle of proportionality to determine a defence to abuse of dominance applies in the assessing of objective justification. As outlined above, although not outlined in our Act, a prima facie abuse is not necessarily an infringement of sections 15 and 16 of the Competition and Consumer Protection if the conduct is objectively justified.

361. Second, the conduct under review must be suitable to achieving the objective. The conduct has 'some relation to the advantages for the market and consumers' - the measure at issue must indeed contribute to achieving the aim pursued.

362. Third, the conduct must not go beyond what is necessary to achieve the objective being pursued. This means that there must be no less restrictive means to achieve the same level of advantages with comparable efforts on the part of the dominant undertaking.

363. Fourth, the Court of Justice in *British Airways* explicitly required a balancing exercise: the advantages must counterbalance or outweigh the disadvantages. And, finally, consumers must benefit.

364. Another defence that could succeed to proving that abuse of dominance is not unlawful is where the enterprise claims the efficiency defence. Under this defence the following have to be satisfied:

- the efficiencies would have to be realised, or be likely to be realised, as a result of the conduct in question;
- the conduct would have to be indispensable to the realisation of those efficiencies;
- the efficiencies would have to outweigh any negative effects on competition and consumer welfare in the affected markets; and
- the conduct must not eliminate all effective competition.

365. It should be noted that this defence is very difficult to prove but could be argued as an objective justification if the above criteria are met.

366. From the above analysis it is clear what the test under section 16 of the Competition and Consumer protection Act is. The test is outlined as follows:

(i) Does the conduct under review prima facie cause competitive harm? The reasonable and proportional pursuit of a legitimate commercial objective is incapable of being even a prima facie abuse;

(ii) If the conduct prima facie causes competitive harm, it is relevant to determine whether:
  - it produces efficiencies (or pursues some other legitimate objective);
  - it is suitable to achieving the efficiencies;
  - it is the least restrictive means of achieving them;
  - the benefits of the conduct, for both producers and consumers, outweigh the potential competitive harm;

- the conduct benefits consumers; and
- whether there is a legitimate defence for the abuse of authority.

367. It is worth noting that sections 15 and 16 of the Competition and Consumer Protection Act do not require a causal link between dominance and abuse. This provision which provides that abuse of domination is outlawed had the objective of protecting undistorted competition in the internal market. Therefore, the strengthening of the dominant position of an undertaking may be an abuse, 'regardless of the means and procedure by which it is achieved', if it has a negative impact on an effective competitive structure. The question of 'the link of causality' was 'of no consequence'.

368. The above means that for an abuse to be established, it is not required that dominance be the 'but for' or *sine qua non* cause of the abusive conduct.

369. While dominance need not necessarily be the means through which the abuse is effected, it is far from clear that the law does not require a link between dominance and abuse. The definition of dominant position in the Zambian Competition Act provides that it is a situation where an enterprise or a group of enterprises possesses such economic strength in a market as to make it possible for it to operate in that market, and to adjust prices or output, without effective constraint from competitors or potential competitors.

370. The court considered that the requirement of a link between dominance and abuse was generally established when the abuse took place on the dominated market, while such a link was 'normally not present where conduct on a market distinct from the dominated market produces effects on that distinct market'.

371. The position, therefore, is that a link is always required not that a link is only required in multi-market abuses. This is consistent with the text of sections 15 and 16 of the Competition and Consumer Protection Act read together with the definition of dominant position in section 3, which prohibits an 'abuse by one or more undertakings of a dominant position' not an abuse by one or more dominant undertakings.

372. Section 16 of the Act is therefore, is not a prohibition of socially harmful conduct that applies only to dominant undertakings but is a prohibition of conduct that is socially undesirable because it is carried out by dominant undertakings. In particular, conduct by a dominant undertaking is prohibited when, by impairing an effective competitive structure, it harms social welfare in the long term.

373. Only undertakings having the ability to restrict effective competition can bring about the type of competitive harm that sections 15 and 16 aims at preventing. This demonstrates that a causal link must exist between dominance and the competitive harm that is relevant under sections 15 and 16 of the Competition and Consumer Protection Act.

374. However, causation cannot be the basis for distinguishing between conduct that is abusive *per se* and conduct that is abusive because of its effects. This distinction would be based on whether market power is the means by which the abuse is committed or the condition for anticompetitive effects to occur in the form of a manipulation of market structure.

375. Tying and refusal to supply would be in the former category, while exclusivity, rebates, or acquisitions of competitors or competing technologies would fall into the latter category. These implications drawn from the causation requirement are not well founded. Whether the dominant undertaking engages in refusal to supply or anticompetitive rebates, the anticompetitive effect is the same: the reduction of competitive pressure causing harm to long-term social welfare.

376. The Competition and Consumer Protection Act clearly considers dominance as a necessary condition for harm to occur but not for the conduct to take place. Any firm can refuse to supply a rival or grant retroactive discounts that result in incremental sales below cost. Dominance is a necessary condition for neither form of conduct. But it is a necessary condition for either form of conduct to reduce competition and harm long-term social welfare within the meaning of sections 15 and 16 of the Act.

377. The above considerations demonstrate that section 16 of the Consumer Protection Act envisages a causal link between dominance and competitive harm. Since the abuse tests under section 16 of the Competition and Consumer Protection Act rely on anticompetitive effects to presume competitive harm, this also means that dominance must be an integral element of the assessment of anticompetitive effects.

378. Lastly, as mentioned previously, statutory monopolies are exempt from the provisions of the Competition and Consumer Protection Act.

§7. Concentrations

379. A concentration arises where a change of control on a lasting basis results from the merger of two or more previously independent enterprises or parts of enterprises, or the acquisition, by one or more persons already controlling at least one enterprises, or by one or more enterprises, whether by purchase of securities or assets, by contract or by any other means, of direct or indirect control of the whole or parts of one or more other enterprises.

380. Mergers or concentration can occur where there is a change in the quality of control of an undertaking: there may be a change from sole to joint control; a change in the identity of the parent companies so that there is a change in the nature of the joint control; and a change from joint to sole control.

381. Mergers and takeovers are permitted provided the companies follow the procedure in the Companies Act and comply with the provisions of the Competition and Consumer Protection Act – such that the merged company must not have an unfair competitive advantage in the industry it operates in.

382. Part XIII of the Companies Act deals with mergers and takeovers under the broad term of amalgamation. Section 282 of the Companies Act provides that two or more companies may amalgamate and continue as one company.

383. Section 284 of the Companies Act provides that the board of directors of each company must adopt a resolution. Such resolution must be made in the best interests of the company and the board must be satisfied that the amalgamated company shall, immediately after the amalgamation, satisfy the solvency test.

§8. Joint Ventures

384. Where firms decide to cooperate, the medium for their collaboration can vary widely from one case to another. For example, firms that cooperate in research and development may simply meet on a periodic basis to discuss matters of common interest; they may share out research work and pool the results; they may establish a committee to oversee the research and development programme; or they may go further and establish a joint venture company to conduct their research and development, while maintaining their independence as producers and suppliers to the market. The same range of possibilities exists in relation to other types of cooperation, for example, on production and commercialisation.

385. The Act provides that a merger occurs where a joint venture (JV) occurs between two or more independent enterprises. The Act does not define the term 'joint venture' nor does it provide express instructions on which joint ventures should be captured. However, not all JVs are subject to merger control. The Commission distinguishes between 'full function' JVs and JVs that are 'auxiliary' to the activities of their parent enterprises.

386. A full-function JV, whose assets or turnover value is above the notification threshold, has to be notified to the Commission as a merger. By definition, such a JV performs on a lasting basis all the functions of an autonomous economic entity, competing with other enterprises in a relevant market, and has sufficient resources and staff to operate independently on the relevant market. Although full-function JVs would generally conduct little business with the parent enterprises, there may be situations in which the JV uses a parent enterprise's networks or outlets to conduct its sales. A full-function JV may also rely entirely for an initial start-up period on sales to its parent enterprises or purchases from them before it can become established independently on the market. The length of the start-up period depends on the characteristics of the market concerned.

387. If the joint venture is established for a short, finite period – for example, in order to construct a specific project such as a power plant – it would not be considered to be long-lasting. An enlargement of the activities of a full-function joint venture may amount to a new concentration, as will a change from being partial-function to being full-function.

388. If the joint venture is not full-function, the possibility remains that it might be subject to section 8 of the Competition and Consumer Protection Act – but the provision will also apply if the fully functional joint venture has the object or effect of restricting or distorting competition.

389. Auxiliary joint ventures fulfil a specific purpose for their parent enterprises, for example, in sales, production or research and development. Such JVs will not be considered as a merger subject to control. However, parties to auxiliary JVs may have to apply to the Commission for authorisation under Part III of the Act.

390. To be full-function a joint venture must be established on a lasting basis; the fact that the parents provide for dissolution of the joint venture, for example, in the event of its failure or fundamental disagreement between them, does not mean that it is not established on a lasting basis.

391. The medium chosen for the horizontal cooperation will not normally affect the legal analysis of an agreement, with one very important exception: where the parties to an agreement establish a joint venture to carry out their objectives, this may amount to a concentration or a relevant merger situation - if so, the joint venture will be considered not under sections 8, 9, 10 or 12 of the Competition and Consumer Protection Act as they would not be distorting or restricting competition.

Chapter 5. Consequences of Violations and Enforcement Institutions

§1. Administrative Enforcement

I. Antitrust Authorities

392. The Competition and Consumer Protection Act establishes a Competition and Consumer Protection Commission which is responsible for investigating contraventions of the Act.

393. According to section 5 of the Competition and Consumer Protection Act, the functions of the Commission are to

- review the operation of markets in Zambia and the conditions of competition in those markets;
- review the trading practices pursued by enterprises doing business in Zambia;
- investigate and assess restrictive agreements, abuse of dominant positions and mergers;
- investigate unfair trading practices and unfair contract terms and impose such sanctions as may be necessary;
- undertake and publish general studies on the effectiveness of competition in individual sectors of the economy in Zambia and on matters of concern to consumers;
- act as a primary advocate for competition and effective consumer protection in Zambia;
- advise Government on laws affecting competition and consumer protection;
- provide information for the guidance of consumers regarding their rights under this Act;
- liaise and exchange information, knowledge and expertise with competition and consumer protection authorities in other countries;
- advise the Minister on agreements relevant to competition and consumer protection and on any other matter relating to competition and consumer protection;
- cooperate with and assist any association or body of persons to develop and promote the observance of standards of conduct for the purpose of ensuring compliance with the provisions of this Act; and
- do all such acts and things as are necessary, incidental or conducive to the better carrying out of its functions under this Act.

394. The Act provides for the setting up of a Competition and Consumer Protection Tribunal to hear appeals against decisions of the Commission.

A. Formation and Composition

395. The Competition and Consumer Protection Commission is made up a Board which consists of

- a representative from the Ministry responsible for commerce;
- a representative of the Attorney General; and
- five other members, with experience and knowledge in matters relevant to this Act, appointed by the Minister.

396. The Board of the Competition and Consumer Protection Commission may, for the purpose of performing its. functions under this Act, constitute a committee and delegate to the committee such functions of the Board as it considers necessary. The Board may appoint as members of a committee, persons who are or are not members of the Board and such persons shall hold office for such period as the Board may determine.

397. The Board shall appoint an Executive Director on such terms and conditions as the Board may determine. The Executive Director shall be the chief executive officer of the Commission and shall be responsible, under the direction of. the Board, for the day-to-day administration of the Commission. The Executive Director shall be an ex officio member of the Board.

398. According to section 7 of the Competition and Consumer Protection Act, the Board may appoint any suitable person to be an inspector for the purposes of ensuring compliance with this Act, on such terms and conditions as the Board may determine. Further, the Board shall provide an inspector with a certificate of appointment in the prescribed form which shall be prima facie evidence of the inspector's appointment as such.

399. The Competition and Consumer Protection Tribunal consists of five part-time members appointed by the Minister under the terms of section 67(1) of the Competition and Consumer Protection Act, as follows:

- a legal practitioner of not less than ten years legal experience, who shall be the Chairperson;
- a representative of the Attorney General, who shall be the Vice Chairperson; and
- three other members who shall be experts, with not less than five (5) years' experience and knowledge, in matters relevant to the Competition and Consumer Protection Act.

400. The Minister may also remove any member of the Tribunal for reasons that are not specified in the Act. The Secretariat of the Tribunal also consists of civil servants working in the Ministry of Commerce, Trade and Industry.

B. Investigating Powers

401. The Competition and Consumer Protection Commission has powers under the Competition and Consumer Protection Act to undertake investigations, on its own initiative or on a complaint made by any person, into contraventions of any provision of the Act. The investigative powers of the Commission have been strengthened under the new Act by the appointment of inspectors, who have statutory powers to conduct dawn raids.

402. The need for due process and transparency in the undertaking of the Commission's investigations is also strongly enshrined in the Act. The Act allows the Commission to negotiate suitable arrangements with enterprises under investigation aimed at ensuring the discontinuance of the practice under investigation at any time during or after an investigation. It also provides for the prohibition through injunctions or staying orders of certain acts pending investigation.

C. Adjudicating Powers (Ascertaining and Sanctioning)

403. The Competition and Consumer Protection Act does not properly outline the adjudicating powers of the Commission beyond outlining that they may issue directions or issue fines.

404. The Competition and Consumer Protection Act provides for Competition and Consumer Protection Commission directions relating to restrictive agreements (of both a horizontal and vertical nature), and relating to distortion, prevention or restriction of competition (i.e., abuse of dominance).

405. The directions may be in the form of written orders and may include requirements that the enterprise to which they are given should:

- Terminate or amend an agreement;
- Cease or amend a practice or course of conduct, including conduct in relation to prices;
- Supply goods or services, or grant access to facilities;
- Separate or divest itself of any enterprise or assets, or;
- Provide the Commission with specified information on a continuing basis.

D. Appeals to the Competition and Consumer Protection Tribunal

406. Whereas the Competition and Consumer Protection Act or regulations do not adequately provide for the adjudicating by the Competition and Consumer Protection Commission – it does outline the procedures for the Competition and Consumer Protection Tribunal in section 70, as well as extensive guidelines in the Competition and Consumer Protection (Tribunal) Rules of 2012.

407. The Competition and Consumer Protection Tribunal is responsible for hearing appeals from the Competition and Consumer Protection Commission. According to Rule 3 of the Competition and Consumer Protection (Tribunal) Rules, an appeal to the Tribunal against an order or direction of the Commission shall be instituted by sending to the Secretariat, seven copies of a written notice of appeal stating:

- the name and address of the appellant and the respondent;
- a copy of the order or direction of the Commission;
- the grounds of appeal;
- the relief sought; and
- the address for service of notices and other documents upon the appellant.

408. A notice of appeal shall be lodged with the Secretariat within thirty days from the date on which the order or direction is made.

409. Thereafter, the Secretariat shall, at least fourteen days before the hearing of the Tribunal, cause the notice of the date, time and place of hearing of the Tribunal to be served on the appellant.

410. The Secretariat may, subject to any direction by the Chairperson, at any time after receiving the notice of appeal or an application, require the appellant or applicant to furnish a statement, in writing, setting out further and better particulars of the grounds on which the appellant or applicant intends to rely and any relevant facts and contentions.

411. Where more than one notice of appeal or application is given to the Secretariat by different appellants or applicants in respect of the same matter, the Secretariat may on its own motion or on application, in writing, by a party to the appeal or application, order that the appeals or applications be consolidated.

412. According to section 70:

- Three members of the Tribunal shall form a quorum.
- Any question at a sitting or meeting of the Tribunal shall be decided by a majority of the votes of the members of the Tribunal at the sitting or meeting and in the event of an equality of votes, the person presiding at the sitting or meeting shall have a casting vote in addition to that person's deliberative vote.
- A party to a hearing of the Tribunal may be represented by a legal practitioner or, if the party so elects, by any other person or in person.
- A decision of the Tribunal shall be in the form of a reasoned judgment and a copy thereof shall be supplied to each party to the proceedings and to every person affected by the decision.
- If a person is present at a meeting of the Tribunal at which any matter is the subject of consideration, and in which matter the person or that person's spouse is directly or indirectly interested in a private capacity, that person shall, as soon as is practicable after the commencement of the meeting, disclose the interest and

shall not, unless the Tribunal otherwise directs, take part in any consideration or discussion of, or vote on, any question relating to that matter.
- A disclosure of interest made under this section shall be recorded in the minutes of the meeting at which it is made.
- The Tribunal may, for the purpose of any proceedings, use such assessors or experts as the Tribunal may determine.
- The Tribunal shall cause to be kept a record of its proceedings.

413. The Tribunal shall hold its proceedings in public but upon. application by a party to the proceedings, direct that proceedings be held in camera.

414. The Tribunal may summon witnesses, call for the production of, or inspection of, books, documents and other things, and examine witnesses on oath, and for those purposes, the Chairperson is hereby authorised to administer oaths.

415. The Tribunal may order the parties or either of them to produce to the Tribunal such information as the Tribunal considers necessary for purposes of the proceedings; or take any other course which may lead to the just, speedy and inexpensive settlement of any matter before the Tribunal.

416. At the hearing at the Competition and Consumer Protection Tribunal:-

- the appellant or applicant shall present the evidence on which the appeal or application is based, as the case may be;
- the respondent shall adduce evidence to rebut the evidence of the appellant or applicant;
- the appellant or applicant may address the Tribunal by way of reply to the respondent's evidence;
- the appellant or applicant and the respondent may call a witness to adduce evidence; and
- both parties may, at the conclusion of the hearing, present oral or written submissions to the Tribunal.

417. The Tribunal shall observe the principles of natural justice and shall hear all the evidence tendered and representations made by, or on behalf of, the parties or application.

418. The Tribunal may receive, as evidence, any statement, document, information or other matter that may assist it to deal effectively with an appeal, whether or not the evidence would be admissible in a court of law. Further, the Tribunal may take judicial notice of any fact.

419. Evidence before the Tribunal may be given orally or, if the parties to the proceedings consent or the Chairperson of the Tribunal so orders, by affidavit. The Tribunal may, at any stage of the proceedings, make an order requiring the personal attendance of any deponent for examination and cross examination.

420. A party may, at any time during the hearing, give to the other party notice to produce any document to which the appeal relates which is in possession of that party. A party to the proceedings shall, on request, produce to the Secretariat, any document or other information which the Tribunal may require and which is in the power of that party to produce, and shall afford to every party to the proceedings an opportunity to inspect those documents or copies of the documents and to make copies of the documents.

421. The Tribunal may, during the hearing, receive such additional information relating to the appeal or application as it may consider necessary to enable it dispose of a matter.

422. Except where these Rules otherwise provide, an application for directions of an interlocutory nature in connection with any proceedings shall, unless otherwise ordered by the Chairperson, be made to the Secretariat. An interlocutory application shall be in writing and shall state the title of the proceedings and the grounds upon which the application is made.

423. Where an interlocutory application is made with the consent of all the parties, the consent shall be in writing and signed by, or on behalf of, the parties. Where an interlocutory application is not made with the consent of every party, a copy shall, before it is made, be served on every other party and the interlocutory application shall state that this has been done.

424. A party who objects to an interlocutory application may, within fourteen days after the service of a copy on the party, send written notice of the objection to the Secretariat and a copy to the applicant.

425. The Secretariat shall, before making an order on an interlocutory application, consider all the objections received in. relation to the interlocutory application and, if any party wishes to be heard, the Secretariat shall give the party and every other party an opportunity to be heard.

426. The Secretariat may, and shall, if required by the applicant or by a party objecting to an interlocutory application under this rule, refer an interlocutory application to the Chairperson for decision.

427. A party aggrieved with a decision of the Secretariat on an interlocutory application under this rule, may appeal to the Chairperson by giving notice in Form I set out in the Schedule, to the Secretariat and to every other party, within fourteen days after. service on the party of the notice of the decision or within such further time as may be allowed by the Secretariat. An appeal from a decision of the Secretariat shall not act as a stay of proceedings unless so ordered by the Chairperson.

428. The powers of the Chairperson under this rule may be exercised and discharged in relation to the application by any member of the Tribunal authorised by the Chairperson.

429. Where the parties agree upon the terms of an order to. be made by the Tribunal, particulars of the terms agreed upon shall be in writing and signed by all the parties, their legal representatives or agents. The parties shall send the terms agreed to the Secretariat, and the Tribunal may make an order in accordance with terms, in the absence of the parties.

430. In relation a decision of the Competition and Consumer Protection Tribunal, these shall be in writing and shall contain the following:

- the finding of the Tribunal on each issue of fact or law raised in the proceedings; and
- the reason for the Tribunal's findings.

431. The decision shall be made by the Tribunal within sixty days after hearing the appeal or application.

432. The Secretariat shall send the decision of the Tribunal to the parties and to the Commission, within seven days of the date of the decision of the Tribunal. The Secretariat shall send a copy of the decision of the Tribunal to the Commission for implementation.

E. Other Institutional Tasks (Consultancy to Parliament/Government)

433. The Commission has wide advocacy responsibilities under the Act. Under section 5(f) of the Competition and Consumer protection Act the Commission is the primary advocate for competition and effective consumer protection in Zambia. It also has the functions of cooperating with and assisting any association or body of persons to develop and promote the observance of standards of conduct for the purpose of ensuring compliance with the provisions of the Competition and Consumer Protection Act.

434. The Commission makes itself visible to the business community and general public through the media (both print and electronic). It engages with the Government in what it is doing through representations on discussions under the auspices of trade negotiation forums such as the World Trade Organization and the Economic Partnership Agreements with the European Union. It also has held joint stakeholder workshops with various organisations such as the Law Association of Zambia, the Zambia Association of Chambers of Commerce and Industry, the Chamber of Mines, the Manufacturers Association, and the Pensions and Insurance Authority. Its other advocacy and awareness work has included the following:

- Publication of a weekly column on competition and consumer issues in The Post newspaper, which has the largest circulation in Zambia;
- Appearing on television, and speaking on the country's two main radio stations, on consumer protection issues;
- Touring the country's nine Provinces on awareness campaigns, and;

– Releasing press releases on case handling. It is also publishing a quarterly newsletter with a wide local and international circulation.

435. The competition authority of Zambia cooperates with other similar agencies worldwide at both multilateral and bilateral levels. The cooperation at a multilateral level is done under the auspices of various international and regional organisations, such as United Nations Conference on Trade and Development (UNCTAD), the International Competition Network, COMESA, SADC, the Southern and Eastern Africa Competition Forum, and the African Competition Forum.

436. The Zambian Competition and Consumer Protection Commission also has received valuable technical assistance from various cooperating partners since its inception. In that regard, UNCTAD's capacity-building and technical assistance programme has played a prominent role.

437. While the Commission is doing a lot in sensitising the business community and general public on competition and consumer protection issues, some stakeholders still feel that not enough is being done. There are concerns that the visibility of the Commission is still low and that the Commission needs to have physical representation in all the major centres of the country.

438. There are also expectations that the Commission should educate and sensitise the business community on various anticompetitive practices and the general implementation of competition policy and law, as well as on its responsibilities to consumers.

439. It is noteworthy that the awareness of consumer issues in Zambia was found to be relatively higher than that of competition issues.

II. Government Direct Enforcement Activities

440. As discussed above, the Competition and Consumer Protection Commission is also tasked with advising Government on laws affecting competition and consumer protection and advising the Minister on agreements relevant to competition and consumer protection and on any other matter relating to competition and consumer protection. These duties which encompass wide powers are very important, demonstrating the huge responsibility handed to the commission.

III. Other Administrative Agencies Applying Antitrust Rules

441. The Competition and Consumer Protection Commission would with other agencies namely the Pensions and Insurance Authority and the Energy Regulation Board to ensure any valid exceptions to particular sectors as envisaged under the Act materialise.

IV. Administrative Fines

442. In relation to restrictive agreements that were discussed above and fall under sections 8 to 10 and 12 of the Competition and Consumer Protection Act, the Commission may in addition to, or instead of, giving a direction, make an order imposing a financial penalty on the enterprise not exceeding 10% of that enterprise's annual turnover during the period of the breach of the prohibition up to a maximum period of five years.

443. The Commission shall not impose a financial penalty unless it is satisfied that the breach of the prohibition was committed intentionally or negligently.

444. A person or an enterprise shall not charge a consumer more than the price indicated or displayed on a product or service. A person who, or an enterprise which, contravenes this provision is liable to pay the Commission a fine not exceeding 10% of that person's or enterprise's annual turnover.

445. Section 82 of the Competition and Consumer Protection Act provides that a person who contravenes a provision of this Act for which a specific penalty is not provided for under this Act, commits an offence and is liable, upon conviction, to a fine not exceeding 100,000 penalty units or to imprisonment for a period not exceeding one year, or both.

446. Where an offence under this Act is committed by a body corporate or unincorporate body, every director or manager of the body corporate or unincorporate body shall be liable, upon conviction, as if the director or manager had personally committed the offence, unless the director or manager proves to the satisfaction of the court that the act constituting the offence was done without the knowledge, consent or connivance of the director or manager or that the director or manager took reasonable steps to prevent the commission of the offence.

V. Administrative Injunctions and Other Restrictive Orders

447. Section 58(1) of the Competition and Consumer Protection Act provides that the Competition and Consumer Protection Commission may, where a restrictive agreement falls within the scope of sections 8, 9, 10 and 12 of the Act give an enterprise such directions, in writing, as the Commission considers appropriate to ensure that the enterprise ceases to be a party to the restrictive agreement.

448. The remedies in merger control that are provided for in the Act are also of both a structural and behavioural nature, and are provided for in the case of both prospective mergers and completed mergers that have been found to result in a substantial lessening of competition.

449. According to section 73(1) of the Competition and Consumer Protection Act, the Competition and Consumer Protection Tribunal may, if a merger is implemented in contravention of this Act order a party to the merger to sell any shares, interest or other assets it has acquired pursuant to the merger; or declare void any provision of an agreement to which the merger was subject.

450. The Tribunal may, in addition to or in lieu of making an order outlined in section 73(1) of the Act as above, direct any firm, or any other person, to sell any shares, interest or assets of the firm if the prohibited practice cannot adequately be remedied in terms of another provision of this Act; or is substantially conducted by that firm previously found by the Tribunal to have been a prohibited practice.

451. The Tribunal may make an order as to costs as it may consider just having regard to the merits of the matter. The costs and charges in connection with proceedings before the Tribunal shall be the costs reasonably incurred by the person in connection with the proceedings or such. part of those costs as is determined by the Tribunal.

VI. Interim Measures

452. The Competition and Consumer Protection Act permits the imposition of interim measures by the Competition and Consumer Protection Commission.

453. According to section 62 of the Competition and Consumer Protection Act, where:

(a) the Commission has reasonable grounds to suspect that an enterprise is a party to a prohibited agreement and has not completed its examination of the matter, but believes that there is the risk of serious or irreparable injury to a particular person as a consequence of the agreement;
(b) an enterprise is a party to an agreement which is subject to review, to a monopoly situation or to a merger, on which the Commission has opened but not completed an investigation, and the Commission is satisfied that:
   (i) there is prima facie evidence that competition is being prevented, restricted, distorted or substantially lessened and that, in consequence, serious or irreparably damage may be caused to a particular person; or
   (ii) the enterprise is taking steps that would effectively pre-empt remedial action being taken that would restore the conditions of competition existing prior to the investigation; the Commission may, in writing, give such directions as it considers appropriate if, as a matter of urgency, it considers it is necessary to do so to:
      (a) prevent serious or irreparable injury to a particular person or category of persons;
      (b) protect the public interest; or
      (c) prevent or pre-empt action being taken by the enterprise under investigation.

454. The Commission shall give an enterprise to which it intends to give a direction under this section an opportunity to make representations before the direction is given.

§2. CIVIL ENFORCEMENT

I. Competent Civil Courts

455. Section 58 (1) of the Competition and Consumer Protection Act states that:

(1) The Commission may, where a restrictive agreement falls within the scope of sections eight, nine, ten and twelve, give an enterprise such directions, in writing, as the Commission considers appropriate to ensure that the enterprise ceases to be a party to the restrictive agreement.

456. The above provision makes it clear that the Competition and Consumer Commission has the power to make a decision in the form of a direction when an agreement is found to amount to a restrictive agreement.

457. A person who, or an enterprise which, is aggrieved with an order or direction of the Commission under this Part may, within thirty days of receiving the order or direction, appeal to the Tribunal. This is provided for in section 60 of the Competition and Consumer Protection Act.

458. Appeals from decisions of the Competition and Consumer Protection Tribunal go the Court of Appeal. This is by virtue of Article 131 (1) (c) of the Constitution, where one decides to appeal, they can only appeal to the Court of Appeal.

459. Therefore, the Court of Appeal is only court competent to hear about anticompletive conduct, on appeal from the Tribunal. The appeal to the Court of Appeal must be made within thirty days from the decision of the Tribunal by one of the parties in the Tribunal.

II. Sanctions

460. The Court of Appeal can set aside the decision of the Tribunal or uphold it. This in practice means that the Court of Appeal can confirm, vary or revise a penalty given for anticompetitive action, or damages, as the case may be.

A. *Nullity*

461. Nullity as a civil sanction is possible as the court has the power to declare any agreement that is contrary to, or violates competition law to be null and void.

As discussed above, the Competition and Consumer Protection Commission is initially tasked with giving a direction following investigations into conduct that violates competition law. Thereafter a party may appeal to the Competition and Consumer Protection Tribunal and thereafter the Court of Appeal, both bodies having the power to nullify any conduct that violates competition law.

B. Damages

462. Where the court deems that damages are an adequate remedy, the court will assess the money value of the loss suffered and to award that sum as damages. Damages are a compensatory remedy to the injured party; punishment of the guilty party is not the object of damages.

463. Section 52 of the Competition and Consumer Protection Act states that in addition to a fine, a person who sells goods that do not conform to the mandatory safety standards for a class of goods will be liable for any loss or damage arising as a result of the lack of conformity of the goods with the relevant standard; or the defect or dangerous characteristic on account of which the goods have been declared unsafe.

464. The penalty depends on the terms of the agreement. The violating party may be required to pay a fixed amount of money as stated in the agreement. Where the value is not stated in the contract, the normal principles of contract law in Zambia apply.

465. The Zambian Supreme Court case of *Finance Bank v. Simataa Simataa,*[56] provides that there are three types of unliquidated damages recognised in Zambian law that will apply where a consultant breaches the terms of the contract: -

- Substantial damages, that are intended to put the innocent party in the position he would have been in had the contact not been breached;
- Exemplary damages, which are a sum awarded which is far greater than the pecuniary loss suffered by the innocent party.
- Nominal damages, which are a small token award where there has been an infringement of a contractual right, but no actual loss has been suffered. In such cases the courts will only award nominal damages to 'mark the fact that there has been a breach of contract'. These are usually capped at ZMW 500 when awarding by the courts.[57]

466. Damages will protect one of three interests, namely an expectation interest, a reliance interest or a restitution interest. The award of any damages should be targeted at one of these interests.

56. SCZ Appeal No. 11/2017.
57. *See Barclays Bank Zambia Plc v. Patricia Leah Chatta Chipepa* Selected Judgment No. 16 of 2017.

467. The upper limit of the damages that could be awarded depends on the nature of the case and the extent to which the Tribunal has failed to meet their obligations or adjudicate correctly and the nature of the loss suffered. The expectation damages for breach seek to restore the innocent party to the same economic position that party would have been in had the contract not been breached.

C. Interim Measures

468. An injunction is an order of the court either compelling a party to take a certain step or steps (mandatory injunction) or restraining a party from taking a specified step or steps (prohibitory). An injunction is therefore an order directing a party, and occasionally, a non-party, to perform a certain act or refrain him from performing a certain act in connection with the ongoing litigation. A *quia timet* injunction is an interim injunction to restrain wrongful acts which are threatened or imminent, but which have not yet been committed.

469. Injunctions may be further classified according to the period of time for which the order is to remain in force. A perpetual injunction is a final judgment, and for that reason is usually granted only after trial on the merits. An interim injunction, by contrast, is a provisional measure taken out at an earlier stage in the proceedings before the court has had an opportunity to hear and weigh fully the evidence on both sides.

470. The power to grant interim injunctions is at the discretion of the court, and this should be exercised reasonably, equitably, and judiciously. The exercise of the discretion is based on sound legal principles. The following are the general principles and guidelines which will be taken into consideration before an injunction is granted:

- The first question to be addressed is whether or not a plaintiff has raised a serious question, deserved to be determined at trial. That is to say, the claim must not be frivolous or vexatious. If the claim is frivolous or vexatious, the interim injunction will be refused at the outset;
- If the Applicant has established a serious question to be tried, the court will then consider whether or not the plaintiff will be adequately compensated by an award of damages. If a plaintiff can be adequately compensated, the interim injunction application ought to fail, however meritorious the claim may be;
- In the event that there is doubt as to the adequacy of damages and the ability of the defendant to pay them if the plaintiff were to succeed at trial, the court will then proceed to the next stage, and consider the balance of convenience
- The balance of convenience test may be expressed in terms of whether the risk of injustice if the interim injunction is refused, outweighs the risk of injustice if the injunction is granted;
- Where the balance of convenience is evenly balanced, the court will generally take such measures as may be necessary to preserve the status quo.

471. A party applying for an *ex parte* interim injunction has a duty to make a full, fair and accurate disclosure of all the material facts to the court. The party must draw the court's attention to the significant factual, legal and procedural aspects of a matter.

472. The duty of disclosure applies not only to material facts known to the plaintiff, but also material facts which he should have known, if he had made proper inquiries.

473. An Interim injunction granted *ex parte*, may on sufficiently cogent grounds be discharged or waived on an application itself made *ex parte*. Further, where an interim injunction has been granted following a full inter partes hearing, there is no jurisdictional bar to the court hearing an application by the enjoined party to discharge it. Applications to discharge an interim injunction are made to the same judge who granted the initial interim injunction.

§3. Criminal Enforcement

I. Criminal Sanctions for Antitrust Violations

474. Imprisonment is a competent penalty that can be given for the following offences under the Competition and Consumer Protection Act:

- Imprisonment of up to two years is possible for a person who delays or obstructs an inspector in the performance of the inspector's functions; refuses to give an inspector such reasonable assistance as the inspector may require for the purpose of exercising the inspector's powers; or gives an inspector false or misleading information in answer to an inquiry made by the inspector.
- Contravention of the rule against entering into horizontal agreements.
- Where a product is sold in Zambia without a label to clearly indicate the product name, the ingredients used in the product, the date of manufacture and expiry of the product, the manufacturer's name, the physical location of the manufacturer, the telephone number and any other contact details of the manufacturer.
- Three years imprisonment is possible where goods are sold below the standard set for the class of goods as set by the Zambia Bureau of Standards.

II. Other Application of Criminal Law to Relevant Conducts

475. The conduct highlighted above is the scope of criminal law in Zambian competition law.

III. Role of Prosecutors

476. The prosecutors in this case are the Competition and Consumer Protection Commission who are given the power to pursue criminal conduct contrary to the Competition and Consumer Protection Act.

IV. Competent Criminal Courts

477. Like with civil cases, the competent court is the Court of Appeal as with competition matters, the Commission renders a decision that can be appealed to the Tribunal and then to the Court of Appeal.

Part II. Application of the Prohibitions

Chapter 1. Restrictive Agreements

478. As discussed above, restrictive agreements are those agreements, decisions or concerted practices that have their object or effect of distorting or restricting competition. The two main types of restrictive agreements recognised in Zambia are horizontal and vertical agreements. This chapter will delve deeper into these.

§1. Horizontal Agreements

479. According to section 3 of the Competition and Consumer Protection Act, a horizontal agreement is

> an agreement between enterprises each of which operates, for the purpose of the agreement, at the same level of the market and would normally be actual or potential competitions in that market.

480. The Act provides that these agreements are per se which means that they are prohibited in all circumstances so that it is not necessary for the Commission to demonstrate that it has anticompetitive effects.

481. According to section 14(1) of the Competition and Consumer Protection Act, where the parties to a horizontal agreement, together supply or acquire 30% or more of goods or services of any description. in a relevant market in Zambia; the parties shall apply to the Commission for authorisation of the agreement in the prescribed manner and form. The Commission shall, upon receipt of an application under subsection (1), carry out an investigation to determine whether the agreement is prohibited under the Competition and Consumer Protection. Act.

I. Cartels

482. A cartel can be defined as a group of apparently independent producers whose goal is to increase their collective profits by means of price-fixing, limiting supply, or other restrictive practices. Cartels typically control selling prices, but some are organised to force down the prices of purchased inputs.

483. Zambia's Competition and Consumer Protection Act takes several measures to deter and forbid cartels. A single entity that holds a monopoly by this definition cannot be a cartel, though it may be guilty of abusing said monopoly in other ways.

484. The Competition and Consumer Protection Commission has extensive guidelines on cartel conduct that should be read in conjunction with the section 9 of the Competition and Consumer Protection Act. According to the guidelines, a cartel exists when enterprises operating independent of each other agree to act together rather than compete with each other. According to the guidelines, a cartel occurs when the enterprises are competitors in the same market.

A. *Price-Fixing*

485. Price-fixing is undoubtedly as having its object of restricting competition and has been aptly placed as the first type of horizontal agreement in the Act. Section 9(1)(a) of the Competition and Consumer Protection Act provides that a horizontal agreement between enterprises is. prohibited per se, and void, if the agreement fixes, directly or indirectly, a purchase or selling price or any other trading conditions. According to the Competition and Consumer Protection's Guidelines on Cartels, price-fixing includes: agreeing minimum prices, an agreed formula for pricing or discounting of good and services, agreed rebates, allowances or credit terms, collusive quotation of good and services.

486. A key principle of section 9(1)(a) of the Competition and Consumer Protection Act is that competing undertakings must determine their conduct and pricing independently. Price-fixing agreements have been held on numerous occasions to have as their *object* the restriction of competition for the purposes of section 9(1)(a) of the Competition and Consumer Protection Act, so that there is no need also to show that they have the effect of doing so.

487. The Competition and Consumer Protection Tribunal in the case of *Top Gear and Nine Others v. Competition and Consumer Protection Commission,*[58] dealt with several garages that engaged in a cartel to deliberately fix trading conditions in the market. The garages in that case were charging customers for obtaining quotations for the repair of motor vehicles.

488. The Tribunal in *Top Gear* was clear that based on the evidence before it, the garages, as competitors contravened section 9(1)(a) of the Competition and Consumer Protection Act. According to the Tribunal, the conduct of the parties involved was a horizontal agreement to directly fix the trading conditions in the market. The charge for obtaining quotations by companies that operate at the same level of the market as competitors was clear evidence that there was a price-fixing agreement.

58. 2012/CPT/003.

489. Parties cannot argue that their price-fixing agreement does not appreciably restrict competition: the case law has decided that it does, provided that the agreement has an appreciable effect on trade between Member States, a conceptually different point.

490. The exchange of information between competitors may be tainted with an anticompetitive object if the exchange is capable of removing uncertainties concerning the intended conduct of the participating undertaking. In that case as was discussed above, mobile telephone operators exchanged information about the remuneration that they intended to pay their dealers for the services that they provided.

491. Further, where information is exchanged between parties regarding future prices or quantities, this is restrictive of competition by object and can constitute either an agreement, decision or concerted practice that is contrary to section 8 of the Act as a whole.

492. It should be noted that repricing communications in which companies discussed price-setting factors relevant to the setting of future quotation prices amount to the object of price-fixing.

493. An agreement not to discount off published prices even though the parties had not expressly agreed on the level of their published prices and an agreement to observe maximum discounts and to offer the same credit terms are also covered by the section 9(1)(a) rule against price-fixing.

494. It is not just blatant price-fixing that is caught, but that section 9(1)(a) of the Competition and Consumer Protection Act will catch any agreement that directly or indirectly distorts or suppresses price competition.

495. Price signalling which refers to a situation in which there is no direct agreement or concerted practice between undertakings to fix prices, nor a systematic exchange of information between them. Rather the firms send signals to one another about their future commercial intentions, for example, through interviews conducted with the media, speeches at conferences or discussions with customers that are relayed back to competitors. This is implicitly not permitted by section 9(1)(a) of the Competition and Consumer Protection Act as it is an indirect form of price-fixing.

496. The medium through which price-fixing is achieved does not affect whether or not section 9(1)(a) of the Competition and Consumer Protection Act applies. Prior consultation on price lists, with a commitment not to submit quotations before such consultation, is prohibited as are restrictions upon advertising, agreements on terms and conditions which limit price competition, agreements on recommended prices, maximum pricing, surcharges, and collective resale price maintenance (which is also prohibited as a vertical agreement).

497. The fact that an undertaking is not active on the cartelised market does not preclude a finding that the undertaking participated in the cartel. Therefore, it is no defence that a participant in a cartel sometimes does not respect the agreed prices.

498. It should also be pointed out that undertaking cannot justify price-fixing by claiming that it did not have a direct effect on the prices paid by consumers. As alluded to earlier, price-fixing agreements are analysed with regards to their object such that there wouldn't be a need to demonstrate their effect if it is shown that it has the object of fixing prices.

499. The *Top Gear* decision shows us that price-fixing in the services sector is also subject to section 9(1)(a) of the Competition and Consumer Protection Act. This means that in the professional services sector, price-fixing is equally restricted.

500. The Competition and Consumer Protection Commission may also examine particularly carefully markets in which price competition is already limited by extraneous factors, in order to ensure that the parties themselves do nothing further to limit competition, and its decision will not be affected by the fact that the state itself sanction or extended the effect of a price-fixing agreement.

B. Market/Client Allocation

501. Competition may be eliminated between independent undertakings in other ways than through direct or indirect price-fixing. One way of doing so is for firms to agree to apportion particular markets between themselves.

502. Section 9(1)(b) of the Competition and Consumer Protection Act provides that a horizontal agreement between enterprises is. prohibited per se, and void, if the agreement divides markets by allocating customers, suppliers or territories specific types of goods or services.

503. Market-sharing agreements are treated as being restrictive by both object or effect, because they are likely to be harmful to the internal market. It should be noted that collective exclusive dealing amounted to conduct which seeks to restrict or distort competition because it had that object or effect.

504. According to the Competition and Consumer Protection Commission's Guidelines on Cartels, actions that fall under section 9(1)(b) of the Act include allocating customers by geographical area, dividing contracts within an area, agreeing not to compete for established customers, agreeing not to produce each other's products or services and agreeing not to expand into the competitor's market.

505. The key is that competitors agree among themselves how the market will operate, rather than allow competitive market forces to work, this action or conduct tends to shelter cartel members from full exposure to market forces, reduces pressure on them to control costs and innovate. These have the effect of harming efficiency in a market economy such as Zambia and eroding the welfare and rights of consumers.

506. A further way in which a cartel might be able to earn supra-competitive profits is by agreeing to restrict its members' output. If output is reduced, price will rise, and this also amounts to price-fixing as well as a violation of section 9(1)(d) which prohibits production quotas.

C. Production/Innovation Limitation

507. Sections 9(1)(d) of the Competition and Consumer Protection Act provides that a horizontal agreement between enterprises is. prohibited per se, and void, if the agreement sets production quotas.

508. The Zambian decision of *Insurers Association of Zambia v. Competition and Consumer Protection Commission* referred to the case the *European Night Services v. Commission*[59] case where that court referred to agreements to control outlets as containing obvious restrictions of competition; the control of outlets is not specifically outlined in a provision similar to Zambia's section 9(1)(d) of the Competition and Consumer Protection Act.

509. But the court presumably had in mind the imposition on distributors of export bans from entity to another, which have consistently been found to have as their object the restriction of competition: nothing could be more obviously inimical to the goal of market integration in Zambia than these kind of restrictions.

510. Apart from agreements directly fixing prices, supra-competitive profits can also be earned in other ways, for example by limiting production, fixing quotas and dividing markets geographically. Similarly restrictive agreements which limit competition in the terms and conditions offered to customers can have this effect.

511. An agreement not to offer discounts is in effect a price restriction, as would be an agreement not to offer credit; it may well exist to buttress a price-fixing agreement. In some market conditions it might be that non-price competition is particularly significant because of the limited opportunities that exist for price cutting; for example, in an oligopolistic market one oligopolist might be able to attract custom because it can offer a better aftersales service or guarantees or a free delivery service.

59. (1998) ECR II-3141.

D. Group Boycott

512. Sections 9(1)(e) of the Competition and Consumer Protection Act provides that a horizontal agreement between enterprises is. prohibited per se, and void, if the agreement sets production quotas or provides for collective refusal to deal in, or supply, goods or services.

513. Group boycotts can also take the form of collusive tendering. Collusive tendering between actual or potential competitors is a practice whereby firms agree amongst themselves to collaborate over their response to invitations to tender.

514. It is particularly likely to be encountered in the engineering and construction industries where firms compete for very large contracts; often the tenderee will have a powerful bargaining position and the contractors feel the need to concert their bargaining power.

515. From a contractor's point of view collusion over tendering has other benefits apart from the fact that it can lead to higher prices: it may mean that fewer contractors actually bother to price any particular deal (tendering itself can be a costly business) so that overheads are kept lower; it may mean that a contractor can make a tender which it knows will not be accepted (because it has been agreed that another firm will tender at a lower price) and yet which indicates that it is still interested in doing business, so that it will not be crossed off the tenderee's list; and it may mean that a contractor can retain the business of its established, favoured customers without worrying that they will be poached by its competitors.

516. At its simplest, the firms invited to tender agree to quote identical prices, the hope being that in the end each will receive its fair share of orders. Level tendering, however, is extremely suspicious and is likely to attract the attention of the competition authorities, so that more subtle arrangements are normally made. The more complicated these are, the greater will be the cost to the tenderers themselves. One system is to notify intended quotes to each other, or more likely to a central secretariat, which will then cost the order and eliminate those quotes that it considers would result in a loss to some or all of the association's members. Another system is to rotate orders, in which case the firm whose turn it is to receive an order will ensure that its quote is lower than everyone else's. Again, it may be that orders are allocated by a trade association that will advise each member how it should proceed.

E. Collusion on Other Objects

517. Sections 9(1)(c) of the Competition and Consumer Protection Act provides that a horizontal agreement between enterprises is. prohibited per se, and void, if the agreement involves bid rigging, unless the person requesting the bid is informed of the terms of the agreement prior to the making of the bid.

II. Information Exchange Practices

518. The use of information is another basis for deducing a concerted practice under section 8 of the Competition and Consumer Protection Act. Where information is exchanged such that it reduces uncertainty in the market, this facilitates collusion and a party who received and acted on such information would be liable.

519. To infringe sections 8, 9 or 10 of the Competition and Consumer Protection Act, there must be an agreement and/or concerted practice between undertakings to exchange information or a decision by an association of undertakings to the same effect. Sharing of information applies to sharing between competitors of 'strategic data', that is to say data that reduces strategic uncertainty in the market.

520. Information is exchanged in various contexts. It is therefore necessary to characterise the exchange of information in order to ascertain whether competition is likely to be harmed.

521. Where an exchange of information forms part of a horizontal cooperation agreement its assessment should be carried out in combination with the assessment of that agreement; an obvious example would be the parties to a production agreement sharing information about costs. Exchanges of information that are necessary for the implementation of research and development or specialisation agreements may benefit from the block exemption for those agreements.

522. The exchange of information was unlawful where it was part of a mechanism for monitoring and/or enforcing compliance with an unlawful cartel agreement. The exchange of information enables members of a cartel to be sure that each of them is complying with the agreed rules. Information exchange can take various forms: data can be directly shared between competitors or indirectly exchanged through a trade association or a third party.

523. A unilateral disclosure of strategic information can give rise to a concerted practice; there is a presumption that, by receiving such information from a competitor, a firm accepts it and adapts its future conduct on the market.

524. Any discussion among competitors about their prices is likely to be regarded as giving rise to an anticompetitive price-fixing agreement. The exchange of information between competitors that identify the future intended prices or quantities of individual firms has as its object the restriction of competition.

525. As highlighted above from the *T-Mobile* case, it is not a defence for an undertaking to argue that it attended a meeting at which prices were discussed, but that it maintained silence throughout the meeting, and gave no indication of its own intentions. Attendance is sufficient to implicate the undertaking in the price-fixing unless it left the meeting and took positive action to 'publicly distance' itself from the unlawful behaviour.

526. Further, where a party received information about future conduct of a competitor and acts on it, they would be liable for engaging in a concerted practice which has as its object or effect, the prevention, restriction or distortion of competition.

527. Even where a company or entity attends a meeting where another entity discloses its plans to its competitors is likely to be a concerted practice even if there isn't an explicit agreement. This was confirmed in the *T-Mobile*[60] case further underscoring that concerted practices do not need actual agreement.

528. Exchanges of information that do not support an agreement that is itself anticompetitive, and that do not concern future prices or quantities, do not restrict competition by object; however, they may do so by effect. This requires a full analysis of the market.

III. Cooperation Agreements

529. Not all contact between competitors is undesirable and anticompetitive.

530. Some horizontal agreements may be beneficial, such as an agreement between pharmaceutical companies to combine their research and development ('R&D') efforts to develop new and better drugs, or between two small businesses to produce products on a joint basis, thereby achieving economies of scale.

A. Research and Development

531. One of the forms in which competition may manifest itself is in the research and development aspects of an undertaking's activities. Sometimes an undertaking may wish to collaborate with its competitors in order to undertake the necessary research and development.

532. The key to defining markets in R&D cases is to identify those products, technologies or R&D efforts that act as a competitive constraint on the parties to the agreement. In some cases innovation leads to the creation of a new product which is merely a slight improvement on an existing one; at the other end of the spectrum an entirely new product may be created that forms a new market.

533. As sections 8 and 9 of the Competition and Consumer Protection Act deals with agreements that seek to distort or restrict competition, research and development agreements that have the following features will not be held to be anticompetitive:

60. (2009) ECR I-4529.

- Research and development agreements that relate to cooperation 'at an early stage, far removed from the exploitation of possible results'.
- Research and development agreements between non-competitors, unless there is a possibility of a foreclosure effect and one of the parties has significant market power with respect to key technology;
- the outsourcing of Research and development to research institutes and academic bodies which are not active in the exploitation of the results.

534. Pure Research and development agreements that do not extend to joint exploitation of the results; such agreements would fall within sections 8 and 9 of the Competition and Consumer Protection Act only where they appreciably reduce effective competition in innovation.

B. Specialisation

535. This area has not been adequately developed or explored under Zambian competition law.

C. Standardisation

536. Standardisation agreements have as their primary objective the definition of technical or quality requirements with which current or future products, production processes or methods may comply including agreements setting out standards on environmental performance.

537. Standardisation agreements may have effects in four markets:

- in the market for the product itself;
- in the technology market where the standard involves the selection of technology;
- in the service market for the setting of standards;
- in the market for testing and certification.

538. As can be seen from the above, standardisation agreements 'usually produce significant positive economic effects' in particular by promoting innovation and ensuring interoperability.

539. However standard-setting and standardisation agreements may harm competition in three ways: a reduction in price competition following anticompetitive discussions; foreclosure of innovative technologies; and the prevention of effective access to the standard. Standards that involve intellectual property rights may in particular lead to foreclosure effects.

540. Agreements that use a standard as part of a broader restrictive agreement aimed at excluding actual or potential competitors restrict competition by object.

Further, agreements to reduce competition by using the disclosure of most restrictive licensing terms prior to the adoption of a standard as a cover for jointly fixing prices are also treated as restrictions by object which is an infringement of section 8 of the Competition and Consumer Protection Act.

541. Agreements requiring members of a standard-setting organisation to sell products only that comply with a standard may, in certain circumstances, restrict competition by object: this is consistent with the Commission's past practice.

542. It is generally accepted that standard-setting agreements that comply with the following criteria will not infringe section 8 of the Competition and Consumer Protection Act if they adhere to ensuring that the procedure for setting the standards is transparent but no party is forced or obliged to comply (unless it is mandated by statute or other legal instrument). Further, participation in the standard-setting should be unrestricted.

543. A standardisation agreement that departs from the principles may be caught by section. 8 of the Competition and Consumer Protection where the members of a standard-setting organisation are not free to develop alternative standards or products, or where access to a standard or to the standard-setting process is limited.

544. Lastly, a standard-setting agreement that clearly discriminates against any of the participating or potential members could lead to a restriction of competition.

D. Joint Production

545. Joint-production agreements include production carried out by a two or more companies that are controlled by one company or jointly controlled and subcontracting agreements from one contractor to another.

546. Vertical subcontracting agreements between enterprises operating at different levels of the market, whilst horizontal production agreement are those between enterprises at the same level.

547. Joint-production agreements are seen as problematic for many reasons. They may lead to a direct restriction of competition between the parties, even if they market the products independently. Second, they may lead to a coordination of the parties' competitive behaviour, in particular when the production agreement leads to a high commonality of their variable costs.

548. Further, production agreements may lead to third parties being foreclosed from a related market; however, it notes that a foreclosure effect is likely only if at least one of the parties has a 'strong market position' in the market where the risks of foreclosure are assessed.

549. Horizontal agreements to fix prices, limit output or to share markets or customers have as their object the restriction of competition and are outlawed by section 9 of the Competition and Consumer Protection Act. However, it goes on to explain that in two situations restrictions concerning output and prices in the context of joint production would not amount to restrictions by object. The first is where the parties agree on the level of output that is the subject matter of the production agreement; the second is an agreement on the prices at which the jointly produced products (and only those products) will be sold, provided that this is necessary for joint production.

550. Production agreements may also have the effect of restricting competition. In such situation it is necessary to consider what the situation would have been in the absence of the agreement – that is to say to identify the counterfactual; if the production agreement enables the parties to enter a market that they would otherwise have been unable to, the agreement will not be found to have as its effect the restriction of competition.

551. Even where the parties have high market shares, a production agreement may not have the appreciable effect of restricting competition where the market is dynamic, that is to say it is one in which entry occurs and market positions change frequently.

552. A production agreement is more likely to restrict competition by effect where it extends to commercialisation of the products rather than being limited purely to production: the nearer the parties' agreement brings them to the consumer, the higher the risk to competition.

E. Joint Purchasing

553. Unless the object or effect is to restrict or distort competition, a cooperative purchasing association, forbidding its members from participating in other forms of cooperation that were in direct competition with it, did not necessarily restrict competition and may even have beneficial effects on competition.

554. Joint purchasing agreements restrict competition by object if they serve as a disguised cartel, however where the parties agree the price to be paid for the products that are the subject of the joint purchasing agreement, this would not amount to a restriction by object: rather an effects analysis would have to be conducted to determine whether any of the concerns expressed above might arise.

555. In determining whether joint purchasing could have the effect of restricting competition it is necessary to look both at the purchasing and the selling markets. The extent of the parties' market power is obviously relevant to any assessment of possible restrictive effects.

556. The main concerns about joint purchasing agreements in the context of Zambian competition law is arises in the purchasers' *selling* market: if they have a significant degree of market power (not necessarily amounting to dominance) in that market, it may be that they will have no incentive to pass on to consumers any lower prices that they extract from their suppliers.

557. Further, if the parties have significant market power in their *purchasing* market, they may force their suppliers to reduce the range or quality of the products they produce. Additionally, where purchasers with buyer power may be able to foreclose competing purchasers by limiting their access to efficient suppliers.

F. Joint Selling

558. Commercialisation agreements. Are those where there is cooperation between competitors in the selling, distribution or promotion of their products. Distribution agreements generally are covered by the regime for vertical agreements, including some non-reciprocal agreements entered into between competitors.

559. The commercialisation agreements most likely to give rise to concern under section 8 of the Competition and Consumer Protection which prohibits restrictive agreements and section 9 which deals with horizontal agreements are those that give rise to horizontal price-fixing.

560. Joint selling is likely to have as its object the restriction of competition, since it eliminates price competition between the parties on substitute products and may also restrict the total volume of products to be delivered by the parties within the framework of a system for allocating orders.

561. There is a concern that reciprocal distribution agreements between undertakings that are active in different geographical markets may be an instrument for market partitioning if they do so in order to eliminate competition between them: such agreements restrict competition by object; while it would be necessary to consider whether a non-reciprocal agreement constitutes the basis for a mutual understanding to avoid entering each other's territory.

562. Joint-selling agreement would not normally restrict competition if it is objectively necessary to allow one party to enter a market it could not have entered individually; it gives an example of consortia projects in which a number of parties participate, where no one firm could compete for the project individually.

§2. Vertical Agreements

563. The Competition and Consumer Protection Act provides that a vertical agreement is an agreement between. enterprises each of which operates, for the purposes of the agreement, at a different level of the production or distribution chain and relates to the conditions under which the parties may purchase, sell or resell certain goods or services.

564. The Act provides that these agreements are per se which means that they are prohibited in all circumstances so that it is not necessary for the Commission to demonstrate that it has anticompetitive effects.

565. As highlighted above, a vertical agreement are agreements between firms at different levels of the market. They may also be unlawful when they could be harmful to competition according to section 10 of the Competition and Consumer Protection Act to the extent that it involves resale price maintenance. The imposition upon distributors and retailers of minimum or fixed resale prices will be held to infringe section 8 or 11 of the Competition and Consumer Protection Act: such agreements are considered to have as their object the restriction of competition.

566. An example would be where a supplier of goods instructs its retailers not to resell them at less than a certain price, a practice often referred to as resale price maintenance. As a general proposition, vertical agreements are much less likely to harm competition than horizontal ones.

567. However, it is not illegal for a supplier or producer to recommend a minimum resale price to the reseller of a good or a service if the supplier or producer makes it clear to the reseller that the recommendation is not binding; and the product has a price stated on it and the words ‘recommended price’ appear next to the stated price.

568. Where the parties to a vertical agreement, individually supply or acquire, at either one of the two levels of the market that are linked by the agreement, 15% or more of goods or services of any description in a relevant market in Zambia; the parties shall apply to the Commission for authorisation of the agreement in the prescribed manner and form. The Commission shall, upon receipt of an application under subsection (1), carry out an investigation to determine whether the agreement is prohibited under the Competition and Consumer Protection. Act.

I. Distribution

A. Exclusive Distributorship

569. Exclusive distribution occurs where a supplier grants exclusive distribution to a distributor for a particular territory: for example, it might appoint X as the exclusive distributor for Kabwe in Central Province and Y as the exclusive distributor for Lusaka in Lusaka Province. The supplier may also agree that it will not sell its products directly into the territories granted to X and Y.

570. An exclusive distribution agreement does not have as its object the restriction of competition, but must be considered in its market context to determine whether it has this effect.

571. The market position of the supplier and its competitors is of 'major importance', since the loss of intra-brand competition is problematic only if inter-brand competition is limited. However, for it to cross the threshold and be considered an unlawful vertical agreement, it the exclusive distributorship must entail resale price maintenance.

572. In the *Puma Energy Zambia PLC v. Competition and Consumer Protection Commission*[61] case, Dana Oil entered into a Distributorship Agreement in which it was agreed that Dana Oil (the Distributor), shall procure the products exclusively from BP Zambia PLC or such other party as BP may nominate from time to time.

573. In this case, the court did not say exclusive distributorships are not permitted but fined the enterprises because they breached a conditional merger which provided that Castro Oil products should be distributed by an independent distributor but in this case Dana was to procure from BP Zambia (which bought Castro) and distribute to the market.

574. The Competition and Consumer Protection Tribunal ordered the distribution in Zambia to remain independent and that Dana Oil procures its Castrol products from BP Africa and BP products from BP Zambia. The entities refused to comply with this order and were fined by the Tribunal.

B. Exclusive Dealing

575. Exclusive dealing or exclusive customer allocation refers to the situation in which a supplier agrees to sell its products to a distributor who will resell only to a particular class of customers.

576. Exclusive dealing insofar as it deals with the allocation of final consumers is unlikely to satisfy the criteria of the legal exceptions to restrictive agreements and is likely to be an unlawful vertical agreement where it involves e-sale price maintenance and has the effect of restricting or distorting competition.

C. Selective Distribution

577. Selective distribution agreements are often deployed by producers of branded products. The producer establishes a system in which the products can be

61. SCZ Appeal No. 172/2015.

bought and resold only by authorised distributors and retailers. Non-authorised dealers will not be able to obtain the products, and the authorised dealers will be told that they can resell only to other members of the system or to the final consumer.

578. Selective distribution systems may restrict intra-brand competition, may foreclose access to the market, and may soften competition and/or facilitate collusion between suppliers or buyers.

579. In determining the application of section 10 of the Competition and Consumer Protection Act to selective distribution agreements, a distinction must be made between a 'purely qualitative' system and a 'quantitative' system; a purely qualitative selective distribution system will not infringe section 10 of the Competition and Consumer Protection Act at all even though, by its very nature, it may involve the restrictions just mentioned. It will only infringe the Act if it involves resale price maintenance.

D. *Franchising*

580. A franchise is an authorisation granted by a government or company to an individual or group enabling them to carry out specified commercial activities, for example acting as an agent for a company's products.

581. Franchise agreements are generally not considered to be anticompetitive and are allowed in Zambia. This is because franchise agreements promote inter-brand competition in circumstances in which the franchisor would not have made the additional investment to expand its business or enter new markets.

582. As a consequence, restrictive clauses that are strictly necessary to protect the know-how and assistance provided by the franchisor are not 'restrictions of competition' within the meaning of restrictive agreement in sections 8, 9, 10 or 12 of the Competition and Consumer Protection Act.

II. Technology Licencing

583. This area has not been adequately developed or explored under Zambian competition law.

A. *Patent Licencing*

584. This area has not been adequately developed or explored under Zambian competition law.

B. Trademark Licencing

585. This area has not been adequately developed or explored under Zambian competition law.

C. Know-How and Trade Secret Licencing

586. This area has not been adequately developed or explored under Zambian competition law.

Chapter 2. Dominant Undertakings' Prohibited Practices

§1. Exploitative Practices

I. Excessive/Unfair Pricing

587. The Zambian Competition and Consumer Protection Commission takes action against excessive pricing as well unfair trading practices in relation to prices. Section 16(2)(f) of the Competition and Consumer Protection Act provides that an abuse of the dominant position occurs where an enterprise charges an excessive price to the detriment of consumers.

588. The test to be applied when determining if the price is excessive is whether the price exceeds what the dominant undertaking would have obtained in the counterfactual world of normal and sufficiently effective competition. The question to ask is whether the price bears no reasonable relation to the economic value of the product or service supplied.

589. The *United Brands* case considered how to calculate excess, where it suggests that this may, among other methods, be determined by comparing the price charged for a product with the cost of its production. The Court provided that:

- is the difference between the costs actually incurred and the price actually charged excessive? and
- if so, is the price that has been imposed either unfair in itself or when compared to competing products?

590. One way of determining whether a price is excessive is to ask whether its price is too great in relation to its cost. This has been recognised in section 16(2)(g) of the Competition and Consumer Protection Act which states that it is an abuse of the dominant position to charge prices above the variable costs. In effect, whether the dominant firm is taking too large a margin or making too much profit amounts to abuse.

591. However, this does not mean that a determination that prices are excessive always requires an examination of the price charged and the cost of production; only that this is one way among others – '*inter alia*' – of answering the question.

592. In some cases a price/cost analysis may not be feasible. In some case the excessive price may have to be assessed, for example, by comparing the disputed price with those in other markets rather than on the basis of profitability.

593. It is because price/cost analysis cannot always produce an answer to the question of whether a price is excessive that the Court of Justice said in *United*

Brands that there might be other ways of determining whether this is the case. Competition authorities have 'a certain margin of manoeuvre' with respect to the methodology to be followed when determining whether a price is excessive, and it may be sensible to combine different methods.

594. In particular, depending on the circumstances of the case, it may be appropriate to proceed on the basis of a comparison of the dominant undertaking's prices with an appropriate comparator, for example, the prices of non-dominant firms, or the dominant firm at a different point of time, or the dominant firm in different geographical markets. Any chosen comparator must be selected in accordance with 'objective, appropriate and verifiable criteria', and the comparison must be made on a consistent basis.

595. Whichever methods of comparison are adopted, there must be a 'significant and persistent' difference between the disputed price and the price that would be expected in a competitive market. Ultimately, the competition authority should have a 'sufficiently complete and reliable set of elements which point in one and the same direction.

596. Having established that a price is excessive, it will be abusive only if it is also 'unfair': according to the case of *United Brands* the price has to either be 'unfair in itself', or when compared to competing products. *United Brands* does not elaborate on these ideas, although they both imply a somewhat subjective assessment for the identification of an abusively high price.

597. As to whether an excessive price is unfair in itself, it is necessary to determine whether the excessive price bears no reasonable relation to the 'economic value' of the product. The economic value of a product in the hands of a purchaser does not always or necessarily correspond to its cost of production plus a reasonable rate of return.

598. An excessive price could be unfair in itself where a dominant firm has charged for a service that a customer neither requested nor received or where it charges an excessive price to impede cross-border trade.

599. The suggestion that a price may be determined as unfair when compared to competing products is somewhat awkward, indeed circular in a case where comparators have been used in the first place to determine whether a price is excessive. Any comparator used for the assessment of whether an excessive price is unfair must be sufficiently similar to the product concerned in order for the comparison to be meaningful.

600. Section 46 of the Competition and Consumer Protection Act provides that a person or an enterprise shall not practice any unfair trading, which as discussed includes excessive pricing. A person who, or an enterprise which, contravenes this is liable to pay the Commission a fine not exceeding 10% of that person's or enterprise's annual turnover or one. hundred and fifty thousand penalty units, whichever is higher.

601. Section 53(1) of the Competition and Consumer Protection Act provides that:

(1) In a contract between an enterprise and a consumer, the contract or a term of the contract shall be regarded as unfair if it causes a significant imbalance in the parties' rights and obligations arising under the contract, to the detriment of the consumer.
(2) An unfair contract or an unfair term of a contract between a consumer and an enterprise shall not be binding.

602. The above provision is clearly that a contract cannot include unfair terms, and where there an unfair term that is part of the contract, it will not be binding. Unfair terms are those which cause a significant imbalance in the rights and obligations arising under the contract, to the detriment of the consumer. This is subject to section 53(3) of the Act which is clear that a contract shall bind the parties if it is capable of being enforced without the unfair term.

603. One of the major prohibitions not permitted under Zambian law is any conduct that amounts to a misrepresentation. The Zambia Court of Appeal in *Thomas Sinkala v. Engen Petroleum Zambia Limited*[62] provided that:

> A representation is a statement made by a representor to a representee and relating to way of affirmation, denial description or otherwise to a matter of fact. The statement may be oral or in writing or arise by implication from words or conduct ...

604. The Court of Appeal in *Pulse Financial Services Limited (t/a Entrepreneurs Financial Centre) v. Elaine Munga, Justine Mpundu and Ernest Phiri*[63] endorsed the definition of a representation as a statement of fact, past or present, as distinct from a statement of opinion or of intention, of law. Thus, if it can be proved that the person who expressed the opinion did not hold it, or could not as a reasonable man having his knowledge of the facts, honestly have held it, the statement may be regarded as a statement of fact.

605. The Court of Appeal in *Elaine Munga*[64] held that party wishing to rely on misrepresentation must ensure that it is clearly and distinctly alleged and at trial must lead evidence to prove the allegation clearly and distinctly. There are a number of essential elements that must be satisfied in order to claim the false statement

62. CAZ Appeal No. 208/2019.
63. CAZ Appeal No. 133/2019.
64. CAZ Appeal No. 133/2019.

as an actionable misrepresentation. Therefore, each of the above requirements must be lucidly pleaded and addressed to succeed.

606. Misrepresentation can therefore be defined according to these essential elements:

(a) a statement that is of material fact, not of law;
(b) which was untrue or falsely or at least incorrectly stated;
(c) made by one party to a contract to the other party to the contract,
(d) before or at the time of making the contract;
(e) the party seeking legal redress must have relied upon and acted upon the misrepresentation when entering into the contract;
(f) which was intended to operate and did operate as an inducement to the other party to enter the contract;
(g) which was not intended to be a binding obligation under the contract; and
(h) the plaintiff must have suffered damage as a result of the misrepresentation.

607. The misrepresentation must be material; it must have induced the reasonable person to enter into the contract. In *Nyimba*,[65] the Supreme Court stated that a misrepresentation must be material, that is to say it should influence a prudent insurer in deciding first whether or not to take up the risk and second, the premium to be fixed for such risk. Further, the representee must also have relied on the statements. It is advanced that there can be no reliance if the representee was not aware of the misrepresentation.

II. Discrimination

608. Price discrimination may be defined as the sale or purchase of different units of a good or service at prices not directly corresponding to differences in the cost of supplying them.

609. Section 45(b) of the Competition and Consumer Protection Act provides that a trading practice is unfair if it compromises the standard of honesty and good faith which an enterprise can reasonably be expected to meet.

610. Further, section 16(2)(c) of the Competition and Consumer Protection Act provides that it is an abuse of dominance to apply dissimilar conditions to equivalent transactions with other trading parties. Based on these provisions, it is clear that price discrimination is not permitted in Zambia.

65. Selected Judgment 12 of 2017.

611. There can be price discrimination both where different, non-cost-related prices are charged for the sale or purchase of goods or services of the same description and also where identical prices are charged in circumstances in which a difference in the cost of supplying them would justify their differentiation.

612. There are many costs involved in supplying goods or services which may result in the charging of differentiated yet non-discriminatory prices. For example, apart from the cost of transporting goods, a manufacturer may incur heavier costs where it has to handle a series of small orders from a particular customer rather than a single, annual one.

613. Price discrimination may be exploitative of customers, for example where higher prices are charged to 'locked-in' customers unable to switch to alternative suppliers; it can also be harmful to the competitive process, where it leads to a distortion of competition in markets downstream of the dominant undertaking. The case law establishes that, in determining whether there is an infringement of sections 16(2)(c) and 45(b) of the Competition and Consumer Protection Act – there are some issues that must be addressed.

614. First, does the accused undertaking have a dominant position? Clearly there can be an infringement of section 16 of the Competition and Consumer Protection Act only if an undertaking has a dominant position, and this would be in the upstream market; there is no need for the firm to be present, still less dominant, in the downstream market.

615. Second, it has to be determined if the dominant enterprise entered into equivalent transactions with other trading parties. It is implicit in section 16(2)(c) of the Competition and Consumer Protection Act that a dominant enterprise must have the benefit of giving same prices and treatment to all. Different treatment must be examined only where compared transactions are 'equivalent'. Factors to be considered in determining whether one transaction is equivalent with another include the nature of the product supplied and the costs of supply.

616. Linked to the above, it has to be determined if the dominant enterprise guilty of applying dissimilar conditions to equivalent transactions. This is quite explicit in section 16(2)(c) of the Competition and Consumer Protection Act.

617. Lastly it needs to be determined if there an objective justification for the discrimination. A dominant firm may be able successfully to argue that discrimination is objectively justified or enhances efficiency. As already noted, differential pricing may increase a dominant firm's output and enable customers to obtain a product which they might not otherwise be able to afford.

618. Section 46 of the Competition and Consumer Protection Act provides that a person or an enterprise shall not practice any unfair trading, which as discussed includes discriminatory pricing. A person who, or an enterprise which, contravenes this is liable to pay the Commission a fine not exceeding 10% of that person's or enterprise's annual turnover or one. hundred and fifty thousand penalty units, whichever is higher.

§2. EXCLUSIONARY PRACTICES

I. Predation

619. Predatory pricing means selling at a loss. This section will examine whether or not this amounts to behaviour that is not permitted by the Competition and Consumer Protection Act.

620. Predatory pricing occurs where a dominant company. sets a price which is below their average variable costs. Where this occurs this amounts to the abuse of the dominant position to undermine or restrict competition and is likely to not be permitted under section 16 of the Competition and Consumer Protection Act, specifically section 16(2)(g) of the Act which provides that an abuse of dominant position includes selling goods below their marginal or variable costs.

621. To this end, it is submitted that a lucid test for predatory pricing is critical. Predatory pricing occurs where a dominant firm deliberately reduces prices to a loss-making level when faced with competition from an existing competitor or a new entrant to the market; the existing competitor having been disciplined, or the new entrant having been foreclosed, the dominant firm then raises its prices again, thereby causing consumer harm.

622. Attempts to eliminate an existing competitor may be more expensive and difficult to achieve than deterring a new one from entry, especially where the existing competitor is committed to remaining in the market.

623. Where a dominant undertaking has a reputation for acting in a predatory manner, this in itself may deter new entrants: not only predatory pricing itself but also the reputation for predation may be a barrier to entry.

624. Dominant firms, like any other, have the right to compete on price. The law on predatory price cutting has to tread a fine line between not condemning dominant firms for competitive price cutting on the one hand while not condoning unreasonable exclusionary predation on the other.

625. Proving intention could be relevant in determining if predatory pricing is an abuse of dominance.

626. It would be wrong to have a *per se* rule that selling at below cost is always illegal. For example, it is arguable that a dominant firm should sometimes be able to sell below cost; sales promotions may involve below-cost selling; and the disposal of old stock at the end of the season at a price below cost would presumably not be unlawful.

627. Separately, it may be possible for a dominant firm to defend prices that would otherwise amount to an abuse on the basis that it was meeting competition. However, the Court of Justice has held that a dominant firm does not have an 'absolute right' to align its prices on those of its competitors where this would mean that it was selling at below cost. Clearly it is necessary to balance the interest of the dominant firm to minimise its losses and the interests of competitors to enter or expand.

II. Tying

628. Tying is the practice of a supplier of one product, the tying product, requiring a buyer also to buy a second product, the tied product. Although it is not put in these exact terms, section 45(c) of the Competition and Consumer Protection Act provides that it is an unfair trading practice to place pressure on consumers by using harassment or coercion. Based on this tying is not permitted in Zambia.

629. The notion of tying is, at first sight, simple enough; a customer is forced to purchase two distinct products that could have been bought individually. However, a moment's reflection reveals that there is a real difficulty in determining when two or more products should be regarded as distinct so that their sale together should be regarded as a tie. This is implied in section 45(a) and (c) of the Competition Act which prohibit trading practices that mislead consumers or places pressure on consumers by use of harassment or coercion. Tying may take various forms.

630. Withdrawal or withholding of a guarantee occurs where a dominant supplier may achieve the effect of a tie by withdrawing or withholding the benefit of a guarantee unless a customer uses a supplier's components as opposed to those of a third party.

631. A refusal to supply has the effect of a tie may be achieved where a dominant undertaking refuses to supply the tying product unless the customer purchases the tied product.

632. Technical tying occurs where the tied product is physically integrated into the tying product, so that it is impossible to take one product without the other.

633. Bundling is closely related to the idea of tying. It refers to a situation in which two products are sold as a single package at a single price. Two types of bundling should be noted:

- pure bundling: this occurs where it is only possible to purchase the two products together;

– mixed bundling: this occurs where the two products are sold separately; however, when they are sold together they are available at a discount to the price that would be charged if they were purchased separately.

634. Further because section 16(2) of the Competition and Consumer Protection Act does not have an exhaustive list of what constitutes abuse of a dominant position, tying could also amount to abuse of the dominant position. In determining whether there is an infringement of section 16 of the Competition and Consumer Protection Act in relation to abuse of dominance, five issues must be addressed:

– Does the accused undertaking have a dominant position? There can be an infringement of section 16 only if an undertaking has a dominant position, and this would be in the tying market; there is no need for dominance in the tied market.
– Has the dominant undertaking tied two distinct products? The notion of tying is, at first sight, simple enough; a customer is forced to purchase two distinct products that could have been bought individually. However, a moment's reflection reveals that there is a real difficulty in determining when two or more products should be regarded as distinct so that their sale together should be regarded as a tie. Products are tied when they have no connection either 'by their nature or according to commercial usage'.
– Was the customer coerced to purchase both the tying and the tied products? a component of the abuse of tying is that the customer is coerced into acquiring the tied product – *making* the conclusion of contracts subject to acceptance by the other parties of supplementary obligations.
– Is the tie capable of having an anticompetitive foreclosure effect? To amount to an abuse tying must have, or be capable of having, an anticompetitive foreclosure effect. The Competition and Consumer Protection Commission discusses factors that it would take into account when deciding whether tying might lead to anticompetitive foreclosure.
– Is there an objective justification for the tie? As was seen above, to avoid liability for abuse of dominance, a dominant undertaking is entitled to demonstrate that tying is objectively justified or enhances efficiency.

III. Rebates

635. Section 16 of the. Competition and Consumer Protection Act does not specifically state that offering rebates to customers is abusive.

636. There are three kinds of rebates in competition law. These are:

– quantity rebates: these are simply linked to the volume of sales to a customer, and the General Court considered them to be presumptively lawful;
– exclusivity rebates: these are conditional on customers buying only from the dominant undertaking and the General Court considered them to be presumptively unlawful unless objectively justified;

- third category rebates: that is to say rebates that are neither quantity nor exclusivity rebates, but which may have a loyalty-inducing effect; these may be unlawful, depending upon an appraisal of all the circumstances of the case.

637. The Competition and Consumer Protection Commission will condemn rebates and similar practices which have the effect of impeding imports and exports. Pricing practices that were intended to dissuade customers from purchasing from other entities are likely to be abusive.

638. The court thereby provided that it was abusive for a dominant undertaking to tie a customer by an exclusive purchasing agreement or by offering fidelity rebates.

639. To determine if rebates are abuse of a dominant position, the Competition and Consumer Protection Commission is required to undertake an economic analysis to determine whether the rebates could have a foreclosure effect. Just like is done in the European union and the United Kingdom, when doing so, the Commission must consider:

- the extent of the dominant firm's position on the market;
- the share of the market covered by the challenged practice;
- the conditions and arrangements for granting the rebates in question; and
- the possible existence of a strategy aiming to exclude as efficient competitors from the market.

640. Further, where the rebates could eliminate an as efficient competitor from the market, it is still possible for the dominant firm to demonstrate that they are objectively justified or that they lead to efficiencies to the benefit of consumers.

IV. Refusal to Deal

641. There are circumstances in which a refusal on the part of a dominant firm to deal or supply goods or services can amount to an abuse of a dominant position.

642. Most refusal to supply cases concern a vertically integrated undertaking that is dominant in an upstream market and which refuses to supply an existing or a new customer in a downstream market on which it is also present.

643. The above appears to establish that, in determining whether a refusal to supply a customer in a downstream market amounts to an abuse of a dominant position, five issues must be addressed:

- Is there a refusal to supply? This includes both refusals to supply and constructive refusals which are an offer of supplies on terms that are unreasonable – 'making an offer you cannot accept.
- Does the accused undertaking have a dominant position in an upstream market?

- Is the product to which access is sought indispensable to someone wishing to compete in the downstream market? A vertically integrated undertaking is not required to deal with customers with which it competes in a downstream market simply because it is dominant in relation to an upstream market. It is necessary that the product or service to which a customer seeks access is 'indispensable' if it is to be able to compete in the downstream market.
- Would a refusal to grant access lead to the elimination of effective competition in the downstream market? Under this requirement, it is not necessary for the Commission to demonstrate that 'all' competition on the market would be eliminated; it was sufficient to show that the refusal to supply is liable, or likely, to eliminate all *effective* competition.
- Is there an objective justification for the refusal to supply? Possible justifications are that: the customer is a bad debtor, has become a credit risk or has failed to observe its contractual obligations; the customer will use the input for an illegal purpose; the dominant firm has capacity constraints that make it impossible for access to be provided; the dominant firm needs to realise an adequate return on investments required to develop its input business or granting access might affect negatively both the dominant firm's incentive to innovate and that of downstream competitors. The existence of an objective justification is ultimately a question of fact to be determined in the particular circumstances of each case. Vague, general and theoretical arguments are insufficient.

644. The input to which access is sought must be something that is incapable of being duplicated, or which could be duplicated only with great difficulty. An input will be indispensable if duplication is:

- physically impossible: for example, there may be only one point on the coastline of a country where a deep-sea port can be established; and planning or environmental reasons may make it impossible to build a competing airport, a nationwide system of gas transportation or a second rail network;
- legally impossible: for example, where an undertaking owns intellectual property rights;
- not economically viable, although the Court of Justice was careful to point out in *Bronner* that it is not sufficient for a small firm to argue that, because of its smallness, it should be entitled to use its larger competitor's infrastructure; rather economic non-duplicability asks whether the market is sufficiently large to sustain a second facility such as the dominant firm's system; this presages the idea of the 'as efficient competitor' test in relation to non-pricing abuses.

V. Price/Margin Squeeze

645. A price or margin squeeze occurs where a firm is dominant in an upstream market and supplies a key input to undertakings that compete with it in a downstream market.

646. In such a situation the dominant firm may have a discretion as to the price it charges for the input, and this could have an effect on the ability of firms to compete with it in the downstream market.

647. In determining whether a margin squeeze amounts to an abuse of a dominant position, five issues must be addressed.

- Is the accused undertaking operating on an upstream and a downstream market?
- Does the accused undertaking hold a dominant position in the upstream market? Sections 15 and 16 of the Competition and Consumer Protection Act only where an undertaking has a dominant position: this would be in the upstream market in margin squeeze cases. It is not necessary to establish a dominant position on the downstream market as well.
- Do the dominant firm's upstream and downstream prices allow an undertaking as efficient as the dominant firm to compete on the downstream market? To determine whether or not a margin squeeze infringes section 16 of the Competition and Consumer Protection Act, the following need to be considered: the absence of any regulatory obligation on the dominant firm to supply the upstream product, the degree of dominance held; the absence of a dominant position on the downstream market; whether the customers to whom the pricing practice is applied are new or existing customers; the inability to recoup losses and the fact that the markets involve new as opposed to established technology.
- Is the margin squeeze capable of producing anticompetitive effects? Implicit in competition law is the need to show that conduct restricts or limits or distorts competition for this reason, proving the conduct of market squeezing produces anticompetitive effects is necessary.
- Is there an objective justification for the margin squeeze?

Chapter 3. Concentrations

648. A concentration arises where a change of control on a lasting basis results from the merger of two or more previously independent enterprises or parts of enterprises, or the acquisition, by one or more persons already controlling at least one enterprises, or by one or more enterprises, whether by purchase of securities or assets, by contract or by any other means, of direct or indirect control of the whole or parts of one or more other enterprises.

649. Mergers or concentration can occur where there is a change in the quality of control of an undertaking: there may be a change from sole to joint control; a change in the identity of the parent companies so that there is a change in the nature of the joint control; and a change from joint to sole control.

650. Mergers and takeovers are permitted provided the companies follow the procedure in the Companies Act and comply with the provisions of the Competition and Consumer Protection Act – such that the merged company must not have an unfair competitive advantage in the industry it operates in.

651. Part XIII of the Companies Act deals with mergers and takeovers under the broad term of amalgamation. Section 282 of the Companies Act provides that two or more companies may amalgamate and continue as one company.

652. Section 284 of the Companies Act provides that the board of directors of each company must adopt a resolution. Such resolution must be made in the best interests of the company and the board must be satisfied that the amalgamated company shall, immediately after the amalgamation, satisfy the solvency test.

§1. Horizontal Mergers

653. Horizontal effects occur where a merger takes place between actual or potential competitors in the same product and geographic markets and at the same level of the production or distribution cycle.

654. The horizontal effects of mergers pose a bigger to danger to competition in Zambia than vertical (or conglomerate) ones, because they involve different entities at the same level rather than in the same supply chain.

655. For this reason, horizontal mergers may be scrutinised both for their 'unilateral' or 'non-coordinated' effects and for their 'coordinated' effects.

§2. Vertical Mergers

656. Vertical effects may be experienced where a merger occurs between firms that operate at different, but complementary, levels of the market for the same final product: for example, A might produce a raw material (an 'upstream' product) for a product produced by B (a 'downstream' product).

657. Often such mergers will enhance, or be neutral, in terms of economic efficiency, but there is a possibility that vertical integration may have a harmful effect on competition, either because it could foreclose access to the market on the. part of third parties or because it could lead to collusion between the merged entity and third parties.

§3. Market/Product Extension Mergers

658. This area is not adequately covered in Zambian competition law.

§4. Pure Conglomerate Mergers

659. There have been a few occasions on which competition authorities have had concerns about mergers not on the basis of horizontal or vertical effects, but because of possible conglomerate effects: for example, that a merger between A and B who are neither horizontal competitors, nor functionally related vertically, might enable the merged entity AB to use its market power in two different but related, or even unrelated, markets to foreclose competitors.

§5. Joint Ventures

660. Two or more enterprises which merge part of their businesses into a newly established joint venture company, may be found to be parties to a merger. In these instances, the enterprises involved have joint control. Joint control occurs where two or more undertakings have the possibility of exercising decisive influence over another undertaking. Joint control typically arises from the fact that the undertakings in question enjoy negative control, that is to say the power to reject strategic decisions, which means that they have to act in common in order to determine the joint venture's commercial policy.

661. Joint control can be established both on a legal and a factual basis. Joint control can arise where:

– there are only two parent companies each with the same number of voting rights;
– In the absence of voting equality, parent companies enjoy veto rights, either by virtue of the statute of the joint venture or a shareholders' agreement between the parents. The veto rights must be related to strategic decisions of the joint venture on issues such as the budget, business plan, major investments or the appointment of senior management; or

– in the absence of veto rights, it is likely, in fact or in law, that the parents will act jointly in the exercise of their voting rights, whether as a result of a legally binding agreement or as a matter of fact, because of ‘strong common interests.

662. A joint venture is one where both parent companies are responsible for its strategic decisions, which is precisely why they will be considered to be in joint control in the first place. To be operationally autonomous the joint venture must have sufficient resources to operate independently on a market: this means that it must have a management dedicated to its day-to-day operations and access to sufficient resources including finance, staff and assets to carry on the business activities provided for in the joint venture agreement.

663. A joint venture will not be full-function where it takes over one specific function of its parents’ activities, such as research and development or production; similarly, a joint sales company would not be full-function.

664. In such an instance, this transaction needs to comply with the Competition and Consumer Protection Act.

Part III. Administrative Procedure

Chapter 1. Administrative Investigations Before the Anti-trust Authority

§1. Initiative

665. Section 55 of the Competition and Consumer Protection Act stipulates that the Competition and Consumer Protection Commission may, at its own initiative undertake an investigation if it has reasonable grounds to believe that there is, or is likely to be, a contravention of any provision of the Competition and Consumer Protection Act.

666. The Commission may, where it undertakes an investigation carry out public consultations on the subject of the investigation in such manner as it considers appropriate.

667. The Commission shall, upon opening an investigation, as soon as practicable, give written notice of the investigation to the person who is the subject of the investigation or to an enterprise which is suspected to be a party to the matter to be investigated and shall indicate in the notice, the subject matter and the purpose of the investigation.

I. General Sectors Inquiries

668. According to the Competition and Consumer Protection Regulations, the Competition and Consumer Protection Commission may initiate a market enquiry based on:

- complaints made to it by enterprises, consumers or representative bodies;
- studies conducted by any relevant bodies on a particular sector;
- its own research;
- its experience in regulating restrictive business and anticompetitive trade practices; or
- representations made to it by the Government regarding a particular sector or type of agreement.

669. When enterprises, consumers or representative bodies ask for a market enquiry, the Commission can only institute the enquiry if they have reasonable grounds to believe that consumers are being treated unfairly by enterprises doing business in that sector with them.

670. Where the Competition and Consumer Protection Commission decides to institute a market inquiry, it is required by Regulation 5 of the Competition and Consumer Protection Regulations to inform the general public about the enquiry by placing a notice on its website or in a daily newspaper of general circulation in Zambia.

671. The Executive Director of the Competition and Consumer Protection Act may appoint a member of staff of the Commission or an inspector as an inquiry manager where the Commission institutes a market enquiry. The inquiry manager appointed is to be in charge of the market inquiry.

672. The Competition and Consumer Protection Commission shall where it receives adverse third-party concerns against an enterprise that it considers to be involved in the matters covered by the market inquiry provide the enterprise with the full details of the adverse concerns, for confirmation.

673. The Commission may, where it determines that a regulated sector is unduly restrictive of competition, conduct a market inquiry into the sector. The Competition and Consumer Protection Commission may initiate a market inquiry where it. has reasonable grounds to suspect that a restriction or distortion of competition is occurring within a particular sector of the economy; or within a particular type of agreement occurring across various sectors.

674. The Minister may, on the advice of the Commission, prescribe the procedure for determining the relevant product market within which the share of supply or acquisition thresholds are to be met under subsection (1) of sections 14 dealing with share of supply threshold for authorisation of restrictive agreements and 15 dealing with share of supply threshold for establishing existence of dominant position.

675. Section 39 of the Competition and Consumer Protection Act outlines the purpose of the market enquiry. According to the provision, the purpose of a market inquiry is to determine:

- whether any feature, or combination of features, of each relevant sector and each type of agreement has the effect of preventing, restricting or distorting competition in connection with the supply or acquisition of any goods or services in Zambia; and
- whether any of the circumstances referred as legal exceptions to restrictive agreements in section 19 of the Competition and Consumer Protection Act, apply to the sector or type of agreement on the same basis as they would have applied to any matter arising under section sixteen.

676. The Competition and Consumer Protection Commission shall, in determining the relevant product market, identify-

- the peculiar appearance, use, price range, quality characteristics, uniqueness and any other feature or characteristic of the product that sufficiently distinguishes it from other products;
- whether targeted consumers consider the product to be different in terms of, among others, benefits, taste or usage, to the extent that it affects purchase decisions;
- whether in the event of a shortage, lack of availability, a price increase or any other constraining factor, another product could be used or substituted by consumers for the same use;
- whether competitors have failed or are likely to fail to supply a similar product:
- the geographical location within Zambian which the bulk of sales or supply of the product take place;
- the historical consumer behaviour, if any, related to the product; and
- the uniqueness of the production process of the product and the ease with which a different production process can be altered to produce the product.

677. The Commission may invite interested parties to submit information to it and may exercise, in relation to any enterprise that it considers to be involved in the matters covered by the inquiry, its powers of investigation under the Competition and Consumer Protection Act.

678. The Competition and Consumer Protection Commission in determining the relevant product market, may use any relevant research findings of third parties, conduct public inquiries, consider or adopt international best practice determinations market definition, insofar as they are consistent with the Act and these Regulations and are practical to the Zambian situation, as it may determine.

679. The Commission shall, at the conclusion of a market inquiry, publish its findings in a daily newspaper of general circulation in Zambia.

680. The Competition and Consumer Protection Commission shall, where it finds as a result of an inquiry that the adverse effects for competition exist in relation to a sector or a type of agreement and that the legal exceptions do not apply, or applies to a limited extent:

- insofar as particular practices identified by the inquiry are capable of being addressed as matters falling within section 8 (1) or section 9 (1) or section 10 (1) or section 16, deal with them in accordance with the provisions of the Competition and Consumer Protection Act relating to such matters; or
- insofar as the adverse effects for competition cannot be remedied under this Act, or are the result of other applicable laws, make recommendations to the Minister for such further action, including amendments to applicable laws as is required to provide an effective remedy.

II. Ex Officio Investigations

681. The Commission may, where it undertakes an investigation carry out public consultations on the subject of the investigation in such manner as it considers. appropriate.

682. The Commission shall, upon opening an investigation, as soon as practicable, give written notice of the investigation to the person who is the subject of the investigation or to an enterprise which is suspected to be a party to the matter to be investigated and shall indicate in the notice, the subject matter and the purpose of the investigation.

III. Complaints

683. Any person who alleges one off the following may lodge a complaint with the Competition and Consumer protection Commission where they believe that a person or an enterprise:

– is practising any unfair trading;
– has made a false or misleading representation in respect of any goods, services or facilities;
– has displayed a disclaimer at any trading premises contrary to the provisions of the Competition and Consumer Protection Act;
– has supplied defective or unsuitable goods or provided. unsuitable services to that person;
– is selling goods that do not conform with the mandatory safety standards for the class of goods;
– has concluded or is enforcing an unfair contract or term of contract to the detriment of that person; or
– has contravened any other provision of this Act relating to consumer protection or has failed to comply with a requirement under the Competition and Consumer Protection Act, to the detriment of that person.

§2. POWERS

I. Requests for Information

684. For the purpose of an investigation under this section, the Commission may, by notice in writing served on any person, require that person to:

– furnish to the Commission, in a statement signed by that person or, in the case of a body corporate, by a director or member or other competent officer, employee or agent of the body corporate, within the time and in the manner specified in the notice, any information pertaining to any matter specified in the notice which the Commission considers relevant to the investigation;

- produce to the Commission, or to a person specified in the notice, any document or article, as specified in the notice, which relates to any matter which the Commission. considers relevant to the investigation; or
- appear before the Commission, or before a person specified in the notice, at a time and place specified in the notice, to give evidence or to produce any document or article specified in the notice.

II. Investigating and Search Powers

685. As mentioned above, the Competition and Consumer Protection Commission may, where it undertakes investigations to assess restrictive agreements, abuse of dominant position and mergers and unfair trading practices and contract terms, as well as carry out public consultations on the subject of the investigation in such manner as it considers. appropriate.

686. The Commission shall, where it receives a request from any person to investigate a matter and determines that a request is frivolous or vexatious, dismiss the request and inform, in writing, that person of its decision and the reasons therefor.

687. An inspector is permitted by section 7(4) of the Competition and Consumer Protection Act to:

(a) enter and search any premises occupied by an enterprise or any other premises, including a private dwelling, where information or documents which may be relevant to an investigation may be kept;
(b) search any person on the premises if there are reasonable grounds for believing that the person has personal possession of any document or article that has a bearing on the investigation: Provided that a person shall only be searched by a person of the same sex;
(c) examine any document or article found on the premises that has a bearing on the investigation;
(d) require information to be given about any document or article by:
  - the owner of the premises;
  - the person in control of the premises;
  - any person who has control of the document or article; or
  - any other person who may have the information;
(e) take extracts from, or make copies of, any book or document found on the premises that has a bearing on the investigation;
(f) use any computer system on the premises, or require assistance of any person on the premises to use that computer system, to:
  - search any data contained in, or available to the computer system;
  - reproduce any record from the data; or
  - seize any output from the computer for examination and copying; and

(g) attach and, if necessary, remove from the premises for examination and safeguarding any document or article that appears to have a bearing on the investigation.

688. An inspector shall, in performing any functions outlined above should be in possession of the certificate of appointment and show the certificate of appointment to any person who requests to see it or is subject to an investigation.

689. A person who delays or obstructs an inspector in the performance of the inspector's functions; refuses to give an inspector such reasonable assistance as the inspector may require for the purpose of exercising the inspector's powers; or gives an inspector false or misleading information in answer to an inquiry made by the inspector; commits an offence and is liable, upon conviction, to a fine not exceeding two hundred thousand penalty units or to imprisonment for a period not exceeding two years, or to both.

690. An inspector shall furnish the Commission with a written report and any other information relating to an inspection, as the Competition and Consumer Protection Commission may require.

691. Sections 55 and 56 of the Competition and Consumer Protection Act regulates investigations by the Competition and Consumer Protection Commission. According to section 55, the Commission may carry out investigations following a complaint by any person, or own its own initiative. Where the Competition and Consumer Protection Commission carries out these investigations, the law requires them to carry out public consultations in such a manner as it considers appropriate.

692. The Commission shall, upon opening an investigation, as soon as practicable, give written notice of the investigation to the person who is the subject of the investigation or to an enterprise which is suspected to be a party to the matter to be investigated and shall indicate in the notice, the subject matter and the purpose of the investigation.

693. According to the Competition and Consumer Protection Tribunal in *Top Gear and Nine Others v. Competition and Consumer Protection Commission,*[66] where the Commission issues a search warrant that complies with section 55 of the Act, they would have complied with the provisions of the law.

III. Cooperation with Other State Institutions

694. The Patents and Companies Registration Agency is very likely to play a role in cooperating with the giving of adequate information and status of any enterprises being investigated.

66. 2012/CPT/003.

IV. Report

695. The Commission shall, at the conclusion of an investigation under this section, publish a report of the inquiry and its conclusions in such manner and form as it considers appropriate.

§3. RIGHT OF DEFENCE

I. Content and Notification of Opening Decisions

696. The Commission may, upon giving notice to persons or enterprises being investigated, invite comments from any party with an interest in the matter under investigation.

697. Further, The Competition and Consumer Protection Commission shall where it receives adverse third-party concerns against an enterprise that it considers to be involved in the matters covered by the market inquiry, provide the enterprise with the full details of the adverse concerns, for confirmation.

II. Proceedings: Hearings, Access to File, Briefs

698. During a market inquiry, an enterprise may at its own request or at the request of the Competition and Consumer Protection Commission, appear before the Commission to make any submission relevant to a market inquiry, before the Competition and Consumer Protection Commission makes its final determination on the market inquiry.

699. Further, section 55 of the Competition and Consumer Protection Act provides that when conducting investigations, the Competition and Consumer Protection Commission may require a person to:

– furnish to the Commission, in a statement signed by that person or, in the case of a body corporate, by a director. or member or other competent officer, employee or agent of the body corporate, within the time and in the manner specified in the notice, any information pertaining to any matter specified in the notice which the Commission considers relevant to the investigation;
– produce to the Commission, or to a person specified in the notice, any document or article, as specified in the notice, which relates to any matter which the Commission considers relevant to the investigation; or
– appear before the Commission, or before a person specified in the notice, at a time and place specified in the notice, to give evidence or to produce any document or article specified in the notice.

700. The Commission may, where it has reasonable grounds to believe that the giving of a written notice as above may materially prejudice its investigation, defer the giving of such notice until after the investigation is concluded. Notwithstanding this, the Competition and Consumer Protection Commission may receive from any person any statement, document, information or article that may assist with its investigation.

III. Statement of Objections

701. A statement of objection is a formal step in Competition and Consumer Protection Commission investigations into suspected violations of the rules in the Competition and Consumer Protection Act. The Commission informs the parties concerned in writing of the objections raised against them.

702. Section 55(3) of the Competition and Consumer Protection Act provides that the Competition and Consumer Protection Commission shall, upon opening an investigation, as. soon as practicable, give written notice of the investigation to the person who is the subject of the investigation or to an enterprise which is suspected to be a party to the matter to be investigated. and shall indicate in the notice, the subject matter and the purpose of the investigation.

IV. Final Hearing and Decision

703. There is no time frame given for when the Commission must make its final decision.

704. The Commission may, where a restrictive agreement falls within the scope of sections 8,9, 10 or 12 considers appropriate to ensure that the enterprise ceases to be a party to the restrictive agreement.

705. Such a direction may require an enterprise to terminate or modify the restrictive agreement concerned within such period as may be specified by the Commission.

706. Further, in addition to, or instead of, giving a direction, the Competition and Consumer Protection Commission may make an order imposing a financial penalty on the enterprise not exceeding 10% of that enterprise's annual turnover during the period of the breach of the prohibition up to a maximum period of five years.

707. The Commission shall not impose a financial penalty unless it is satisfied that the breach of the prohibition was committed intentionally or negligently. An order imposing a penalty shall be in writing and shall specify the date by which the penalty is required to be paid.

708. Where the Commission determines, after review, that an enterprise is a party to a restrictive agreement referred to under sections 8, 9, 10 or 12 or that it is a party to a dominant position within the terms of section 16, and that:

(a) in relation to the restrictive agreement, the agreement. has the object or effect of preventing, restricting or distorting competition; or
(b) in relation to the dominant position, any conduct of the. enterprise:
    (i) has the object or effect of preventing, restricting or distorting competition; or
    (ii) in any other way, constitutes exploitation of the monopoly situation, the Commission may give the enterprise such directions as it considers necessary, reasonable and practicable to:
        (a) remedy, mitigate or prevent the adverse effects on competition that the Commission has identified; or
        (b) remedy, mitigate or prevent any detrimental effects on users and consumers so far as they have resulted from, or are likely to result from, the adverse effects on, or the absence of, competition.

709. The Commission may, at any time, during or after an investigation under this Part, enter into a consent agreement with an enterprise under investigation or request the enterprise to give an undertaking in the prescribed manner and form.

710. In relation to mergers, the Competition and Consumer Protection Act provides that the Commission may, where it determines after an investigation that an enterprise is a party to a merger and the creation of a merger has resulted, or is likely to result, in a substantial lessening of competition within a market for goods or services, give the enterprise such directions as it considers necessary, reasonable and practicable to remedy, mitigate or prevent the substantial lessening of competition; and remedy, mitigate or prevent any adverse effects that have resulted from, or are likely to result from, the substantial lessening of competition.

711. The Competition and Consumer Protection Commission may, in the case of a prospective merger require an enterprise to

- desist from completion or implementation of the merger insofar as it relates to a market in Zambia;
- divest such assets as are specified in a direction within the period so specified in the direction, before the merger can be completed or implemented; or
- adopt, or desist from, such conduct, including conduct in relation to prices, as is specified in a direction as a condition of proceeding with the merger.

712. Section 61(3) of the Competition and Consumer Protection Act provides that the Commission may, in the case of a completed merger, require an enterprise to:

- divest itself of such assets as are specified in a direction within the period so specified in the direction; or
- adopt, or to desist from, such conduct, including conduct in relation to prices, as is specified in the direction as a condition of maintaining or proceeding with the merger.

713. The Commission shall keep under review the compliance with directions given by it and the performance of undertakings given by an enterprise.

714. The Competition and Consumer Protection Commission is mandated by section 5(d) of the Competition and Consumer Protection Act to investigate unfair trading practices and unfair contract terms and impose such sanctions as may be necessary and by section 5(1) of the Competition and Consumer Protection Act to do all such acts and things as are necessary, incidental or conducive to the better carrying out of its functions under the Act.

715. Further, in terms of section 79 of the Competition and Consumer Protection Act, the respondent may operate a leniency programme where an enterprise that voluntarily discloses the existence of an agreement that is prohibited under the Act, and cooperates with the respondent in the investigation of the practice, may not be subject to all or part of a fine that could otherwise be imposed under the Act.

716. It is clear that the Competition and Consumer Protection Commission has inherent power, in appropriate cases, to impose a fine on an offending enterprise without recourse to the Competition and Consumer Protection Tribunal.

717. It should be noted that section 57 of the Competition and Consumer Protection Act provides that the Competition and Consumer Protection Commission may, at any time, during or after an investigation, enter into a consent agreement with an enterprise under investigation or request the enterprise to give an undertaking in the prescribed manner and form.

718. The Commission shall, upon entering into a consent. agreement with an enterprise, or receiving an undertaking from an enterprise, submit the consent agreement or undertaking, as the case may be, to the Competition and Consumer Protection Tribunal for confirmation. A person who, or an enterprise which, fails to comply with any conditions stated in a consent agreement or with any undertaking given by the person or the enterprise is liable to pay the Commission a fine not exceeding 10% of that person's or an enterprise's annual turnover.

719. Lastly, section 82 of the Competition and Consumer Protection Act, provides for a general penalty to the effect that a person who contravenes a provision of the Act for which no specific penalty is provided for under the Act, commits an offence and is liable, upon conviction, to a fine not exceeding 100,000 penalty units or to a term of imprisonment of up to one year or to both.

V. Variation of the Final Order of the Commission and Ensuring Compliance

720. Section 63(2) of the Competition and Consumer Protection Act provides that the Competition and Consumer Protection Commission may, where it is satisfied that there has been a material change of circumstance agree to vary or terminate a direction; or accept a variation to an undertaking, or release an enterprise from an undertaking.

721. According to section 64 (1) of the Competition and Consumer Protection Act, where the Commission determines that an enterprise has failed, without reasonable cause, to comply with a direction or undertaking, it may, subject to subsection (2), apply to the Tribunal for a mandatory order requiring the enterprise to make good the default, i.e., remedy the breach of competition law, within a time specified in the order.

722. What section 64(1) of the Competition and Consumer Protection Act emphasises is that where an enterprise has failed without reasonable cause to comply with a direction or undertaking, the respondent may apply to the Competition and Consumer Protection Tribunal for a mandatory order requiring the enterprise to make good the default within a specified time.

723. According to the Supreme Court in *Puma Energy Zambia PLC v. Competition and Consumer Protection Commission*,[67] section 64 (1) of the Competition and Consumer Protection Act uses the word 'may' and under the rules of statutory interpretation, the word 'may' connotes discretion or choice between two alternatives.

724. The Commission shall consider any representations an enterprise wishes to make before making an application to enforce compliance with a direction or undertaking in terms of section 64(1) of the Competition and Consumer Protection Act.

725. In *Puma Energy Zambia PLC v. Competition and Consumer Protection Commission*,[68] the court emphasised that the requirement to consider representations from enterprises when seeking to enforce a direction or undertaking is mandatory.

67. SCZ Appeal No. 172/2015.
68. SCZ Appeal No. 172/2015.

Chapter 2. Voluntary Notification and Clearance Decisions

726. The Commission may, at any time, during or after an investigation under this Part, enter into a consent agreement with an enterprise under investigation or request the enterprise to give an undertaking in the prescribed manner and form.

727. The Commission shall, upon entering into a consent agreement with an enterprise, or receiving an undertaking from an enterprise under subsection (1), submit the consent agreement or undertaking, as the case may be, to the Tribunal for confirmation.

728. The Tribunal may, upon receipt of the consent agreement or undertaking under section 57 (2):

(a) give or withhold its confirmation; or
(b) return the matter to the Commission with an indication of any changes that need to be made to the consent agreement or undertaking before the Tribunal confirms it.

729. An undertaking confirmed by the Tribunal shall:

(a) be published by the Commission in the form of a decision of the Commission; and
(b) have effect as if it were a direction of the Commission under section 59.

Chapter 3. Merger Control

730. There are many reasons why the Zambian governments, firms, shareholders, employees and individuals might object to mergers. A Government may object to a merger on a number of grounds: for example, it might disapprove of a foreign firm taking over a native one, or of a merger that does not fit with its own industrial policy, or of a transaction that would lead to production facilities being closed down leading to unemployment.

731. A firm might object to being the target of a hostile bid, or to a merger between two rivals that might give them a competitive edge. Shareholders (whether legal or natural persons) might be concerned that corporate transactions will have an adverse effect on the value or effectiveness of their shares.

732. Merger control is necessary to prevent the creation or strengthening of market power before it occurs, given that there are legal controls namely section 16 of the Competition and Consumer Protection Act on the abuse of market power. Merger control in Zambia is not simply about preventing future abuses but also about maintaining competitive markets that lead to better outcomes for consumers.

733. Further, investigations into the unilateral conduct of dominant firms are lengthy, complex and cumbersome, and that competition authorities lack the resources to police every alleged infringement; exclusive reliance on *ex post* control would be unlikely to be effective.

734. For the purposes of the Competition and Consumer Protection Act, section 24(1) provides that a merger occurs where an enterprise, directly or indirectly, acquires or establishes, direct or indirect, control over the whole or part of the business of another enterprise, or when two or more enterprises mutually agree to adopt arrangements for common ownership or control over the whole or part of their respective businesses.

735. All transactions where an enterprise, directly or indirectly, acquires or establishes direct or indirect control over the whole or part of the business of another enterprise, or when two or more enterprises mutually agree to adopt arrangements for common ownership or control over the whole or part of their respective businesses are captured as mergers. Such transactions include amalgamation or combination of enterprises, joint venture mergers or acquisition of interest in another enterprise, for instance, acquisition of shares, assets or leases, etc.

736. A merger transaction requires authorisation by the Zambian Competition and Consumer Protection Commission where the combined turnover or assets, whichever is higher, in Zambia of the merging parties is at least 50 million fee units in the merging parties' most recent financial year in which these figures are available. 50 million fee units is equivalent to ZMW 15 million. There are circumstances, however, in which transactions falling below the above thresholds may be investigated. The Commission may, where it has reasonable grounds to believe that a merger falls below the prescribed thresholds, review the merger if the following factors exist:

- the merger is likely to create a position of dominance in a localised product or geographical market;
- the merger is likely to contribute to the creation of a dominant position through a series of acquisitions that are not individually subject to prior notification;
- the merger may substantially prevent or lessen competition;
- the merger is concluded outside Zambia and has consequences in Zambia that require further consideration; or
- as a result of the merger there are, or are likely to be, competition and public interest factors that must be considered.

737. In *Rumpuns Trading Limited v. Consumer Protection Commission*,[69] the Competition and Consumer Protection Tribunal dealt with a merger where Prime Time Holdings Limited through its Zambian subsidiary purchased PwC Office Park for USD 8.8 million in Lusaka from Rumpus Trading Limited. It was submitted that this sale occurred without authorisation. The tribunal stated that the purchase of assets falls within the definition of control and requires merger approval in terms of the Competition and Consumer Protection Act.

§1. Preliminary Filing Obligations

I. Criteria and Thresholds

738. Per section 24(2) of the Competition and Consumer Protection Act, a merger may be achieved in the following circumstances:

- where an enterprise purchases shares or leases assets in, or acquires an interest in, any shares or assets belonging to another enterprise;
- where an enterprise amalgamates or combines with another enterprise; or
- where a joint venture occurs between two or more independent enterprises.

739. According to section 24(3) of the Competition and Consumer Protection Act, a person controls an enterprise if that person:

- beneficially owns more than one-half of the issued share capital of the enterprise;
- is entitled to vote a majority of the votes that may be cast at a general meeting of the enterprise, or has the ability to control the voting of a majority of those votes, either directly or through a controlled entity of that enterprise;
- is able to appoint or to veto the appointment of a majority of the directors of the enterprise;
- is a holding company and the enterprise is a subsidiary of that company;

69. 2017/CCPT/019/COM.

- in the case of an enterprise which is a trust, has the ability to control the majority of the votes of the trustees, to appoint the majority of the trustees or to appoint or change the majority of the beneficiaries of the trust;
- has the ability to materially influence the policy of the enterprise in a manner comparable to a person who, in ordinary commercial practice, can exercise the element of control referred to above; or
- has the ability to veto strategic decisions of the enterprise such as the appointment of directors, and other strategic decisions which may affect the operations of the enterprise.

740. In *Rumpuns Trading Limited v. Consumer Protection Commission*,[70] the Competition and Consumer Protection Tribunal stated that the concept of control in section 24(3) should not be accorded a literal interpretation as this would result in a weak safeguard against anticompetitive mergers. In that case, the court stated that an interpretation that excludes control over acquired assets is untenable.

741. Filing is mandatory only in relation to the mergers that meet the notification requirements. A filing is not mandatory in the case of a transaction that does not meet the prescribed threshold. However, a party seeking clarification as to whether a proposed merger is required to be notified may apply to the Commission for negative clearance in the prescribed manner and upon payment of the prescribed fee.

742. The Act does not impose deadlines for filing and the Commission has in certain instances accepted notifications made after conclusion. The Act prohibits the implementation of a merger without obtaining merger approval.

743. There are sanctions for not filing a merger application. These sanctions include an administrative penalty not exceeding 10% of the annual turnover of the enterprise. Not filing a merger application is also a criminal offence that attracts a general penalty; any person who is involved in the implementation of such a merger commits an offence and is liable, upon conviction, to a fine not exceeding 100,000 penalty units (equivalent to ZMW 30,000) or to imprisonment for a period not exceeding one year, or both.

744. Any party to the transaction or the parties' appointed representatives can notify the Commission and pay filing fees. The parties may lodge a joint notification (which is the option preferred by the Commission), but if there are two or more independent parties intending to take over a competitor separately then each party is required to lodge a separate notification.

745. The application fee payable in respect of notifiable mergers is 0.1% of the combined turnover or assets, whichever is higher. The combined turnover or assets refers to the combined annual turnover or combined assets of the entity located in Zambia in which the target entity has an interest. The notification fee is based on

70. 2017/CCPT/019/COM.

the total values of the turnover or assets of the economic entity in Zambia, even if proportions of these amounts are generated outside the market for the merger assessment (i.e., it is the position of the Commission that if a merging party has subsidiaries located in Zambia they form a single economic unit). For parties wholly domiciled outside Zambia, the notification fee will be based on the total values of the turnover generated in Zambia. The ceiling on the filing fee is ZMW 5 million.

746. There is no prescribed waiting period, but there is an initial assessment period of ninety days for authorisation of the merger, which runs from the date of notification to the Commission for the grant of approval. The Commission may extend the assessment period by a period not exceeding thirty days after it gives notice fourteen days prior to the expiry of ninety days.

747. If the Commission does not issue its determination regarding a proposed merger within the period specified, the proposed merger shall be deemed to be approved.

748. The implementation of the transaction has to be suspended while awaiting clearance.

749. The notification is required to be detailed enough for the Commission to be able to make a preliminary assessment with a view of authorising the merger. The notification is made on a prescribed Form 1 as well as a Supplementary Information Request form, which are fairly detailed. Form 1 specifies the following documents to accompany the application:

- two copies of the latest annual report and audited accounts (including the balance sheet);
- a copy of the agreement or other documents relating to the transaction;
- a press release or other shareholders, board or management statement on the transaction;
- other market or industry study reports that support the transaction; and
- strategic plans or minutes of the board on the transaction.

750. Notwithstanding the above, supplementary information requests may be done prior to assessment and during assessment if need be. Further, applicants for merger approval may have pre-notification meetings with the Commission to, *inter alia*, determine the information actually required by the Commission and may result in a significant reduction in the information required to be submitted. The Commission may, at any time, revoke an approved merger if a party to the merger submitted materially incorrect or misleading information in support of the merger.

II. Market Assessment

751. The Competition and Consumer Protection Commission shall, upon receipt of a proposed merger notification, carry out a market assessment of the proposed merger to determine the likely effects of the proposed merger in the relevant market, on trade and the economy, in general. This is carried out in terms of section 29 of the Competition and Consumer Protection Act.

752. Any party to a merger transaction seeking clarification as to whether the proposed merger requires the authorisation of the Commission under section 26 or is subject to review by the Commission under section 27 of the Competition and Consumer Protection Act, may apply to the Commission for negative clearance in the prescribed manner and form upon payment of the prescribed fee.

753. Regulation 9 of the Competition and Consumer Protection Regulations provides that such an application must be set out in the prescribed form.

III. Turnover Calculation

754. The Minister may, by statutory instrument, on the recommendation of the Commission, prescribe the threshold to be applied for the purposes of determining if an authorised merger should be permitted.

755. According to the Competition and Consumer Protection Regulations, merger transactions require authorisation by the Competition and Consumer Protection Commission where the combined turnover or assets, whichever is higher, in Zambia, of the merging parties, is at least 50 million fee units in their latest full financial year, for which figures are available.

756. To this end mergers enquire approval from the Competition and Consumer Protection Commission and they apply guidelines from the Competition and Consumer Protection Act and its regulations.

757. According to section 29 of the Competition and Consumer Protection Act, the Commission shall, upon receipt of a proposed merger notification, carry out a market assessment of the proposed merger to determine the likely effects of the proposed merger in the relevant market, on trade and the economy in general.

IV. Market Share Calculation

758. Most mergers cause no harm to competition. However, there are cases where it can be predicted that the merger will change the structure of the market in ways that provide the merged entity with the incentive and the ability to exercise market power. The Competition and Consumer Protection Commission is concerned about a particular merger which will need to articulate its theory as to how competition will be harmed.

759. Any system of merger control must set a substantive test against which to determine whether a particular merger should be modified or prohibited. To this end, section 27 of the Competition and Consumer Protection Act provides that the Competition and Consumer Protection Commission may, where it has reasonable grounds to believe that a merger falls below the prescribed threshold, review the merger if:

- the merger is likely to create a position of dominance in a localised product or geographical market;
- the merger is likely to contribute to the creation of a dominant position through a series of acquisitions which are not individually subject to prior notification;
- the merger may substantially prevent or lessen competition;
- the merger is concluded outside Zambia and has consequences in Zambia that require further consideration; or
- as a result of the merger, there is, or is likely to be, competition and public interest factors which require to. be considered.

760. What is important during assessing these factors in section 27 is that merger assessment necessarily involves predicting the effect on competition in the market if a particular transaction is consummated.

761. The above necessarily involves a comparison between the situation if the merger goes ahead and the position if it did not happen, the competitive situation without the merger is often referred to as the counterfactual.

762. The counterfactual will usually be the prevailing conditions before the merger, although there may be cases in which it is necessary to take into account conditions as they would be in the near future if, for example, it is known that other firms are about to enter or exit the market or to expand capacity; another example would be that one of the merging firms was on the point of failing, so that it would not be present on the market in the future anyway.

763. The theory of harm, which is the starting point for any merger investigation, is whether the merger is likely to prevent or lessen competition in the relevant market. In a merger assessment, the Commission will generally consider the basic theories of harm, namely unilateral or monopolisation effects, coordinated effects and non-horizontal (foreclosure) effects. Market dominance and vertical foreclosure are important factors and are frequently referred to in most merger investigations, particularly with respect to vertically integrated undertakings.

764. As can be seen from the above, section 27 of the Competition and Consumer Protection Act seeks to protect and guard against the various effects of mergers on competition. These effects are the vertical effect, coordinated effect, unilateral effect and conglomerate effect.

A. *Vertical Effect*

765. As a general proposition it is unlikely that a merger will produce adverse vertical effects. Indeed, a merger between an upstream firm, for example X, with a downstream firm, Y firm for example, is likely to be neutral in terms of economic efficiency or even highly beneficial. For example, if X and Y are independent each will need to earn a margin on its operation – perhaps corpus Firm as a producer and Chibesakunda Firm as a distributor.

766. The merged XY Firm will need to earn only one margin: the elimination of 'double marginalisation' may lead to lower costs, and therefore to lower prices for the customers of XY Firm. However, there may be circumstances in which a vertical merger may harm competition, first, where it forecloses other firms in the industry from entering the market and, secondly, where the vertical integration of Corpus Chibesakunda Firm makes it more likely that there will be coordinated effects on the market.

767. An example of foreclosure could arise where X Firm, a firm in an upstream market, acquires access through a merger with Y Firm, a firm in a downstream market, to an important downstream product, for example, a distribution system such as a gas pipeline that is difficult to duplicate.

768. The merged entity XY Firm may have the incentive to deny competitors in the upstream market access to the distribution system, thereby foreclosing them from the downstream market. Similarly, where Y Firm, a firm in a downstream market, merges with X Firm, a firm that has substantial market power in relation to an important raw material or input in an upstream market, the merged entity XY Firm may have the incentive to deny competitors in the downstream market access to that input. The concern here is that competitors in the downstream market will be unable to obtain supplies of the raw material or input, or that they will be able to do so only on discriminatory terms, with the result that they will be unable to compete effectively.

769. A merger of vertically related firms might also increase the possibility of the merged entity, XY Firm, being able to coordinate its behaviour with other competitors if, for example, it will lead to increased price transparency or if it will make it easier to detect firms that deviate from the coordinated behaviour.

770. In considering whether a merger could give rise to adverse vertical effects a competition authority should not only consider whether the merged entity would have the ability and the incentive to exercise market power; it should also consider carefully whether this would lead to harm to consumers, taking into account in particular the possibility that the merger may give rise to significant economic efficiencies that might be passed on to them in lower prices.

B. Coordinated Effects

771. Coordinated effects occur where, for example, A merges with B and this results in a situation where AB will be able, or more able than when A and B were independent, to coordinate their competitive behaviour on the market with other firms, for example with C and D, and thereby exercise collective market power.

772. Three conditions must be met for coordination to be successful:

- First it must be possible for A, B and C to coordinate their behaviour in some way, for example, by charging the same prices or, perhaps, by aligning their behaviour on output and capacity expansion.
- Second, it must be costly for those firms to deviate from coordination, for example, because 'cheats' will be punished.
- Third, A, B and C must be free from competitive constraint from other participants in the market.

C. Unilateral or Non-coordinated Effects

773. Unilateral effects occur where, for example, A merges with C and the merged entity, AC, will be able, as a result of the merger, to exercise market power. The most obvious manifestation of the exercise of market power is the ability to increase price, but there are other possibilities: for example, a reduction of output, quality, variety or innovation.

774. The 'price increase' includes all these different manifestations of the exercise of market power. The ability to exercise market power is particularly likely if, prior to the merger, an increase in price on the part of A would have been likely to cause a substantial number of customers to divert their purchases to C: post-merger AC would not lose any profits as a result of such a shift, since AC would benefit from the increased sales of B's products. Economists use 'diversion ratios' between A and C to estimate this effect.

775. It may even be that, after the merger, B, a competitor of AC, will also be able to exercise market power because, if AB were to raise its prices, some customers would divert to B, which in turn could raise its own prices. B may be able to do this without coordinating its behaviour with that of AB, in which case B's behaviour can itself be characterised as unilateral or non-coordinated. This is the phenomenon sometimes known as 'non-collusive oligopoly'.

D. Conglomerate Effects

776. As a general proposition conglomerate mergers are unlikely to give rise to adverse competitive effects. They do not involve the removal of actual or potential competitors from the market as in the case of horizontal mergers; nor do they bring together firms that have a vertical relationship in relation to the same final product, where there may be incentives to foreclose competitors from the upstream or downstream market.

777. Furthermore, as in the case of vertical mergers, conglomerate mergers often result in efficiency gains, for example, where the merged entity Corpus Chibesakunda Firm is able to offer complementary products that do not compete with one another to a customer desiring both: if A produces widgets and B blodgets, a 'one-stop shop' may be highly beneficial to a customer that requires both products.

778. The theory of harm in the case of conglomerate effects is particularly speculative – for example that A might decide to 'tie' the two complementary products together in a way that will foreclose competitors, or to price a bundled package of both of them to similar effect. It is possible that tie-in transactions and bundling practices would violate laws that forbid the abuse of a dominant position although the law on this subject is controversial in itself.

V. Investigation

779. Section 61(1) of the Competition and Consumer Protection Act provides that the Competition and Consumer Protection Commission may, where it determines after an investigation that an enterprise is a party to a merger and the creation of a merger has resulted, or is likely to result, in a substantial lessening of competition within a market for goods or services, give the enterprise such directions as it considers necessary, reasonable and practicable to remedy, mitigate or prevent the substantial lessening of competition; and remedy, mitigate or prevent any adverse effects that have resulted from, or are likely to result from, the substantial lessening of competition.

780. Section 61(3) of the Competition and Consumer Protection Act provides that the Commission may, in the case of a completed merger, require an enterprise to:

- divest itself of such assets as are specified in a direction within the period so specified in the direction; or
- adopt, or to desist from, such conduct, including conduct in relation to prices, as is specified in the direction as a condition of maintaining or proceeding with the merger.

781. The Commission shall keep under review the compliance with directions given by it and the performance of undertakings given by an enterprise. Section 63(2) of the Competition and Consumer Protection Act provides that the Competition and Consumer Protection Commission may, where it is satisfied that there has been a material change of circumstance agree to vary or terminate a direction; or accept a variation to an undertaking, or release an enterprise from an undertaking.

782. According to section 64 (1) of the Competition and Consumer Protection Act, where the Commission determines that an enterprise has failed, without reasonable cause, to comply with a direction or undertaking, it may, subject to subsection (2), apply to the Tribunal for a mandatory order requiring the enterprise to make good the default within a time specified in the order.

783. The Commission shall consider any representations an enterprise wishes to make before making an application to enforce compliance with a direction or undertaking in terms of section 64(1) of the Competition and Consumer Protection Act.

784. In the landmark Zambian Supreme Court case of *Puma Energy Zambia PLC v. Competition and Consumer Protection Commission*,[71] section 61 empowers the Competition and Consumer Protection Commission where it determines after an investigation that an enterprise is a party to a merger or the merger created will result in substantial lessening of competition in the market for goods or services to give the enterprise such directions it considers necessary, reasonable and practical.

785. According to the Supreme Court in *Puma Energy Zambia PLC v. Competition and Consumer Protection Commission*,[72] section 64 (1) of the Competition and Consumer Protection Act uses the word 'may' and under the rules of statutory interpretation, the word 'may' connotes discretion or choice between two alternatives.

786. Therefore, section 64(1) of the Competition and Consumer Protection Act which states that the Commission may apply to the Tribunal for a mandatory order is not mandatory to the extent that unless the Commission obtains the order, it cannot proceed to fine an erring enterprise or enforce the fine. The Competition and Consumer Protection Commission is empowered to impose financial penalties including those falling under section 37 of the Competition and Consumer Protection Act, which deals with offences relating to mergers, without recourse to any Court or Tribunal.

787. The above is true, unless on appeal; and that the use of the word 'may' in section 64 entails that the Competition and Consumer Protection Commission has the discretion either to apply for a Mandatory Order from the Tribunal for the enterprise to make good of the default within a certain time or to proceed to fine under section 37 of the Competition and Consumer Protection Act.

788. The wording of sections 37, 61 and 64 of the Competition and Consumer Protection Act which are set out in full above are clear and unambiguous. The sections do not prescribe any particular order in which they should be applied by the

71. SCZ Appeal No. 172/2015.
72. SCZ Appeal No. 172/2015.

respondent and the words used in section 37 of the Competition and Consumer Protection Act do not, in any slightest sense, suggest that before invoking this section recourse must be had to the Competition and Consumer Protection Tribunal or a Court of competent jurisdiction.

VI. Foreign to Foreign Mergers

789. Foreign-to-foreign mergers that have an indirect or direct effect on the structure of local markets are notifiable.

790. The Competition and Consumer Protection Commission focuses on foreign-to-foreign mergers where the merging foreign entities have a subsidiary or interest in an undertaking operating or located in Zambia. An enterprise in Zambia that comes within the control of a foreign enterprise will be subject to notification and review as far as the operation has an effect on competition in Zambia. In such a case, the turnover or assets that will be assessed will be those of an enterprise present (i.e., the enterprise is duly registered in accordance with Zambian law and generates turnover within Zambia) or with a presence in Zambia (i.e., the enterprise is not duly registered in accordance with Zambian law but has sales in Zambia).

791. In the event that the control of a Zambian enterprise comes about purely as a result of a merger or acquisition involving enterprises wholly domiciled outside Zambia, the Commission will nonetheless assess the merger if it has a local nexus. The Commission will only assert jurisdiction over such transactions if the foreign enterprise has a local nexus of sufficient materiality, such as having subsidiaries in Zambia or having made 10% of its sales in Zambia over the last three years.

792. Where an initial assessment reveals no competition concerns, the Commission as a matter of course issues interim authorisations and this enables the parties to close before final clearance by the Board of the Commission (the Board). An interim authorisation is only issued when the Commission is satisfied that a notified transaction gives rise to no competition concerns and it can be reviewed before the final authorisation being granted. The Commission may also require parties to make such undertakings that, in the opinion of the Commission, may remedy any competition concerns to which a notified merger may give rise.

VII. Other Relevant Notions

793. Any party to a merger transaction seeking clarification as to whether the proposed merger requires the authorisation of the Commission under section 26 or is subject to review by the Commission under section 27 of the Competition and Consumer Protection Act, may apply to the Commission for negative clearance in the prescribed manner and form upon payment of the prescribed fee. A negative clearance refers to a certification by the Competition and Consumer Protection Commission that an otherwise anticompetitive conduct can be allowed under conditions.

794. Regulation 9 of the Competition and Consumer Protection Regulations provides that such an application must be made in the Form set out and is termed as a negative clearance.

795. The Commission, in considering a proposed merger, shall according to section 30 of the Competition and Consumer Protection Act, assess whether the merger is likely to prevent or substantially lessen competition in a market in Zambia.

796. Section 30(2) of the Competition and Consumer Protection Act clearly provides that the Commission shall in considering a proposed merger, take into account the likely and actual factors that affect competition in a defined market, including:

- the levels of concentration of players in the relevant market;
- the creation or strengthening of barriers to market entry;
- the level of imports in the relevant market;
- the extent to which there is countervailing buyer or supplier power in the relevant market;
- the availability of substitute products in the relevant market;
- the likelihood of the merger removing from the market an existing effective and vigorous competitor;
- the dynamic characteristics of the market including growth, innovation, pricing and other inherent market characteristics; and
- the risk that a position of dominance may be abused.

797. The Commission may, in considering a proposed merger, conduct a public interest assessment, by taking into account any factor which bears upon the public interest in the proposed merger, including:

- the extent to which the proposed merger is likely to result in a benefit to the public which would outweigh any detriment attributable to a substantial lessening of competition;
- the extent to which the proposed merger would, or is likely to, promote technical or economic progress and the transfer of skills, or otherwise improve the production or distribution of goods or the provision of services in Zambia;
- the saving of a failing firm;
- the extent to which the proposed merger shall maintain or promote exports from Zambia or employment in Zambia;
- the extent to which the proposed merger may enhance the competitiveness, or advance or protect the interests, of micro and small business enterprises in Zambia;
- the extent to which the proposed merger may affect the ability of national industries to compete in international markets;

- socio-economic factors as may be appropriate; and
- any other factor that bears upon the public interest.

798. Even though there is no definition in the Act of what 'public interest' is, it is said to include the extent to which the proposed merger is likely to result in a benefit to the public that would outweigh any detriment attributable to a substantial lessening of competition. There is no exhaustive list of factors that fall under the public interest test, but fundamentally issues such as employment and the effect of the proposed merger on the economy in the relevant market or region affected by the merger are of paramount consideration.

799. As part of its investigation process, the Commission typically conducts public consultations seeking the comments of relevant industry players and other stakeholders with respect to proposed mergers. To the extent that competitors and customers are consulted, competitors and customers play a role in the review process. The Act does not define the meaning of 'public' and therefore both customers and competitors are captured under the Act.

800. Lastly, there are no guidelines in the Act with regard to ancillary restraints and the Commission has not laid down any administrative rules regarding the treatment of ancillary restraints in merger assessments. In practice, clearance decisions will only cover ancillary restraints in circumstances where such ancillary restrictions raise competition concerns as a consequence of which behavioural or structural conditions are imposed. Where a decision is silent on ancillary restraints, they are implicitly cleared.

§2. Structure of Proceedings

I. Preliminary Assessment and Full Investigation

801. The Commission may, after the completion of an assessment and consideration of any representations on a proposed merger:

- approve the proposed merger without any conditions;
- approve the proposed merger with conditions or undertakings given by the parties to address competition and other concerns that may have arisen during the assessment of the proposed merger; or
- reject the proposed merger.

802. The *Puma Energy* case is an example of where the Commission approved a proposed merger with conditions. In that case, a condition set when BP Zambia was to merge with Castro Oil was that Castro branded products should be distributed in Zambia by an independent distributor. BP breached this agreement when it agreed that Dana Oil (the Distributor), shall procure the products exclusively from BP Zambia PLC or such other party as BP may nominate from time to time. The enterprises were fined for this.

803. An officer of the Commission who wishes to undertake an investigation under the Competition and Consumer Protection Act needs to apply to the Competition and Consumer Protection Commission Executive Director for authorisation of the investigations.

804. The Board of the Competition and Consumer Protection Commission may appoint any suitable person to be an inspector for the purposes of ensuring compliance with this Competition and Consumer Protection Act, on such terms and conditions as the Board may determine.

805. An inspector appointed by the Competition and Consumer Protection Commission's Board. may, with a warrant, at any reasonable time:

- enter and search any premises occupied by an enterprise or any other premises, including a private dwelling, where information or documents which may be relevant to an investigation may be kept;
- search any person on the premises if there are reasonable grounds for believing that the person has personal possession of any document or article that has a bearing on the investigation provided that a person shall only be searched by a person of the same sex;
- examine any document or article found on the premises that has a bearing on the investigation;
- require information to be given about any document or article by the owner of the premises; the person in control of the premises; any person who has control of the document or article; or any other person who may have the information;
- take extracts from, or make copies of, any book or document found on the premises that has a bearing on the investigation;
- use any computer system on the premises or require. assistance of any person on the premises to use that computer system, to:
  (i) search any data contained in, or available to the computer system;
  (ii) reproduce any record from the data; or
  (iii) seize any output from the computer for examination and copying; and
- attach and, if necessary, remove from the premises for examination and safeguarding any document or article that appears to have a bearing on the investigation.

806. Inspectors also have the powers to attach and, if necessary, remove from the premises for examination and safeguarding any document or article that appears to have a bearing on the investigation. An inspector who removes any document or article from any premises shall issue a receipt for the document or article to the owner of, or person in control of, the premises; and return the document or article as soon as practicable after achieving the purpose for which it was removed.

807. Should the Commission determine that a merger has resulted or is likely to result in a substantial lessening of competition within a market, it may give an enterprise such directions as it considers necessary to remedy the adverse effects on competition. In the case of a prospective merger, the Commission may require an enterprise to divest such assets as are specified in a direction within the period so specified in the direction, before the merger can be completed or implemented. In the case of a completed merger, the Commission may require an enterprise to divest itself of such assets as are specified in a direction within the period so specified in the direction.

808. The case of *Lublend Limited* represents a merger evaluation combining behavioural and divestiture remedies. In this case, the Commission required the acquiring firm to restructure Lublend Limited so as to allow one of the shareholders to increase its stake to 50%. The acquiring firm was also required to undertake not to interfere with the fixing of blending fees in relation to non-shareholders. In addition, the acquiring undertaking was required to give undertakings that it would facilitate free access to blending facilities by its competitors.

809. This case does not represent a standard approach of the Commission as it evaluates each merger on its own merits and there are no standard conditions or remedies applicable to all cases. For this reason, there are equally no set timelines applicable to all remedies.

II. Time Framework

810. The Commission shall complete its assessment of a proposed merger and issue its determination within a period of ninety days from the date of the application for authorisation of the proposed merger, unless a party to the proposed merger fails to provide the Commission, during the period of assessment, information that is required for the completion of the assessment.

811. Where the Commission does not issue its determination regarding a proposed merger, within the period specified, the proposed merger shall be deemed to be approved.

812. An approval of a merger by the Competition and Consumer Protection Commission does not and shall not relieve an enterprise from complying with any other applicable laws in the Republic of Zambia.

813. The Commission may, at any time, revoke an approved merger if a party to the merger submitted materially incorrect or misleading information in support of the merger; or a party to the merger fails to comply with any condition of an approval of the merger.

III. Right of Defence

814. The Act does not provide for a right of defence beyond appealing the decision of the Commission to the Competition and Consumer Protection Tribunal.

§3. Clearance and Conditional Clearance

I. Conditions and Undertakings

815. The Commission may, according to section 33 of the Competition and Consumer Protection Act, consider any undertakings offered by a party to a proposed merger, in order to address any concern relating to the proposed merger that has arisen, or may be expected to arise, during the assessment of the proposed merger.

A. Content

816. The board of directors of each company which is to be amalgamated shall, not less than thirty days before the amalgamation is proposed to take effect, send to each shareholder:

- a copy of the proposal for amalgamation;
- copies of the declarations made by the directors in compliance with section 284;
- a summary of the principal provisions of the articles of the company;
- a statement:
  (i) that a copy of the articles of the proposed amalgamated company shall be supplied to a shareholder who requests it;
  (ii) setting out the rights of shareholders; and
  (iii) of any material interests of the directors, whether in that capacity or otherwise.

817. The board of directors are also required to send a copy of the proposal to amalgamate to every creditor and give public notice of the proposed amalgamation.

818. After the above provisions are met, the proposal to amalgamate shall be approved by special resolution of the shareholders of each amalgamating company to be amalgamated and the board shall lodge all the documents with the Registrar of Companies who then issues a certificate of incorporation for the new company.

B. Timing

819. The timing for the requirements under the Companies Act are within thirty days of the amalgamation.

§4. Relations with Other Merger Control Authorities

I. Other Authorities Within the Local Jurisdiction

820. The other authorities that deal with mergers are the Patents and Companies Registration Agency (PACRA).

821. Companies that merge must comply with the requirements in the Companies Act and file the relevant resolution and documents with the agency, including permission to merge from the Competition and Consumer Protection Commission at PACRA, within the agreed timeframes.

II. International Coordination

822. According to section 65 of the Competition and Consumer Protection Act, a foreign competition authority may, where it has reasonable grounds to believe that anticompetitive practices in Zambia are damaging competition in the country of the authority, request the Competition and Consumer Protection Commission to investigate and make an appropriate determination.

823. The above applies:

- to requests from other members of the Common Market for Eastern and Southern Africa or of the Southern African Development Community by virtue of the obligations assumed by Zambia towards these organisations; and
- where the Minister has certified by order, in the Gazette, that Zambia has entered into an agreement with one or more States or organisations whereby, on a basis of reciprocity, each party to the agreement shall exercise the principle of comity on the basis described in investigating and determining cases falling within its jurisdiction.

824. The Commission is a member of the International Network of Competition Authorities. Therefore, the Commission may be requested by a foreign competition authority to investigate and make an appropriate determination where it has reasonable grounds to believe that anticompetitive practices in Zambia are damaging competition in the foreign country. The Act also provides for cooperation.

825. The Commission cooperates with antitrust authorities in other jurisdictions. This is supported by a statutory provision in the Act. The Commission can enter into a formal agreement with an authority from a different jurisdiction. This cooperation has been reflected in a number of agreements to which Zambia is a party. For instance, in the 2002 Southern African Customs Union Agreement, the 2009 Southern African Development Community Declaration on regional cooperation in competition and consumer policies, and the 2004 COMESA Competition Regulations, which all provide for cooperation between Member States in the area of competition law enforcement. In January 2013, the Common Market for Eastern and Southern Africa (COMESA) Competition Commission (CCC) became operational and administers the COMESA Competition Regulations and the Commission is expected to cooperate with the Competition and Consumer Protection Commission.

§5. Remedies in Merger Control

826. Section 37 of the Competition and Consumer Protection Act provides that an enterprise which intentionally or negligently implements a merger that is reviewable by the Competition and Consumer Protection Commission without the approval of the Commission; implements a merger that is rejected by the Commission; or fails to comply with conditions stated in a determination or with undertakings given as a condition of a merger approval; commits an offence and is liable to a fine not exceeding 10% of its annual turnover.

827. According to the Supreme Court in *Puma Energy Zambia PLC v. Competition and Consumer Protection Commission,*[73] section 37(c) of the Competition and Consumer Protection Act empowers the Competition and Consumer Protection Commission where an enterprise intentionally or negligently fails to comply with conditions stated in a determination or undertaking to fine the erring enterprise. According to the Supreme Court, it is very clear that the respondent has been given administrative powers under section 37 of the Act to impose a fine not exceeding 10% of its annual turnover for an offence relating to mergers without first applying to the Tribunal for a Mandatory Order of compliance.

828. If the Commission is satisfied that an enterprise investigated for and found to be in violation of section 8 did not intentionally (mens rea) or negligently commit the breach, the Commission shall not impose a financial penalty as provided by subsection (3).

829. The Competition and Consumer Protection Commission may, in the case of a prospective merger require an enterprise to:

- desist from completion or implementation of the merger insofar as it relates to a market in Zambia;
- divest such assets as are specified in a direction within the period so specified in the direction, before the merger can be completed or implemented; or
- adopt, or desist from, such conduct, including conduct in relation to prices, as is specified in a direction as a condition of proceeding with the merger.

§6. Winding up Where the Shareholders in a Merger Do Not Agree with One Another

830. Under section 57(1)*(g)* of the Corporate Insolvency Act, minority shareholders of a company or indeed any party may petition the court, including one of the shareholders after a merger for an order for the compulsory winding up under the Insolvency Act on the ground that it is just and equitable.

73. SCZ Appeal No. 172/2015.

831. Since the just and equitable ground to wind up a company is a very drastic measure, the person petitioning for the liquidation of the company must produce strong grounds to convince the court to invoke this section.

832. The five just and equitable grounds to wind up a company after a merger are if there is:

- is a justifiable loss of confidence in the company's shareholders,
- deadlock in management;
- a director or shareholder has been expelled from management;
- failure of the substratum; and
- unjust management and conduct of the company.

Chapter 4. Challenging of the Administrative Decision

§1. Competent Courts

833. The Competition and Consumer Protection Act has made provisions for an appeal to the Competition and Consumer Protection Tribunal. Therefore, any person or an enterprise that is aggrieved with an order or direction of the Commission may appeal to the Tribunal within thirty days. Any person wishing to appeal against the decision of the Tribunal may appeal to the High Court within thirty days of the determination, and thereafter to the Court of Appeal and finally the Supreme Court.

834. There are recent examples where parities to a merger action aggrieved by the decision of the Commission have appealed to the Competition and Consumer Protection Tribunal (the Tribunal).

835. An appeal to the Tribunal against an order or direction of the Commission shall be instituted by sending to the Secretariat, seven copies of a written notice of appeal stating: (a) the name and address of the appellant and the respondent; (b) a copy of the order or direction of the Commission; (c) the grounds of appeal; (d) the relief sought; and (e) the address for service of notices and other documents upon the appellant.

836. The Competition and Consumer Protection Secretariat may, subject to any direction by the Chairperson, at any time after receiving the notice of appeal or an application, require the appellant or applicant to furnish a statement, in writing, setting out further and better particulars of the grounds on which the appellant or applicant intends to rely and any relevant facts and contentions.

837. The Tribunal shall hold its proceedings in public, and three members of the Tribunal shall constitute a quorum. The Tribunal may, during the hearing, receive such additional information relating to the appeal or application as it may consider necessary to enable it dispose of a matter.

838. The Tribunal may receive, as evidence, any statement, document, information or other matter that may assist it to deal effectively with an appeal, whether or not the evidence would be admissible in a court of law. The Tribunal may take judicial notice of any fact.

839. Evidence before the Tribunal may be given orally or, if the parties to the proceedings consent or the Chairperson of the Tribunal so orders, by affidavit. The Tribunal may, at any stage of the proceedings, make an order requiring the personal attendance of any deponent for examination and cross examination.

840. A party may, at any time during the hearing, give to the other party notice to produce any document to which the appeal relates which is in possession of that party. A party to the proceedings shall, on request, produce to the Secretariat, any document or other information which the Tribunal may require and which is in the power of that party to produce, and shall afford to every party to the proceedings an opportunity to inspect those documents or copies of the documents and to make copies of the documents.

841. The judicial system in Zambia has various levels, starting with the lower courts and rising up to the Supreme Court and the Constitutional Court. The lower courts are the local courts and Magistrates Courts, while the higher courts are the High Court of Zambia, the Court of Appeal, the Supreme Court of Zambia, which is the highest court in Zambia for non-constitutional matters and the Constitutional Court which is the highest court for constitutional matters.

842. A court of competent jurisdiction shall have jurisdiction over any person for any act committed outside Zambia which, if it had been committed in Zambia, would have been an offence under this Act.

843. The High Court as constituted by the Constitution is established as the High Court of Judicature for Zambia by section 3 of the High Court Act.[74] It is a Superior Court of Record that, in addition to any other jurisdiction conferred by the Constitution or any other law, possesses and exercises the entire jurisdiction, powers and authorities vested in the High Court of Justice in England.[75]

844. It has unlimited jurisdiction which includes the judicial hearing and determination of matters in difference, the administration or control of property of persons, the power to appoint or control guardians of infants and their estates, and also keepers of the persons and estates of idiots, lunatics and persons of unsound mind who are unable to govern themselves and their estates.[76]

845. Having unlimited jurisdiction, the High Court can also hear and determine industrial and labour relations cases even though the law has granted jurisdiction in these matters to competition law.

846. Article 130 of the Constitution establishes a Court of Appeal that has jurisdiction to hear appeals from all divisions of the High Court and other courts, except for matters under the exclusive jurisdiction of the Constitutional Court. The Court of Appeal is a new court established by the Constitution (Amendment) Act.[77]

847. Therefore, the Court confirmed that an appeal from the high Court shall lie to the Court of Appeal as this is what the Constitution provides and all law must comply with the Constitution.

74. Chapter 27 of the Laws of Zambia.
75. In the case of *Rahim Obaid v. The People (2) Nadehim Quasmi v. The People* (1977) ZR 119 (HC), it was held that in the absence of any practice and procedure in our laws on the issue, our courts will follow the Practice and Procedure of the High court in England.
76. Section 9 (2).
77. No. 2 of 2016.

848. In the case of *Wilson Masauso Zulu v. Avondale Housing Project Limited,*[78] the Supreme Court made it clear that when a party appeals to the Supreme Court:

> The appellate Court would only reverse findings of fact made by a trial Court if it is satisfied that the findings in question were either perverse or made in the absence of any relevant evidence or upon a misapprehension of facts.

849. The *Zulu* case is also important because the Supreme Court stated that a plaintiff must prove his case even if the defendant has failed to prove his.[79] In *Amiran Limited v. Bones,*[80] the Supreme Court held that an appeal shall not be permitted if it is on points of fact only.

850. It is crucial that when an employee or employer decides to appeal from the decision of the Industrial Relations Court, they apply for a stay of execution of judgment. A stay of execution suspends the operation of the judgment until the appeal is heard. In *Sonny Paul Mulenga and Vismer Mulenga, Chainama Hotels Limited and Elephants Head Hotels Limited v. Investrust Merchant Bank,*[81] the court held as follows:

> an appeal does not automatically operate as a stay of execution, and it is utterly pointless to ask for a stay solely because an appeal has been entered. More is required to be advanced to persuade the court below or this court that it is desirable, necessary and just to stay a judgment pending appeal. In exercising its discretion whether to grant a stay or not, the court is entitled to preview the prospects of success of the proposed appeal.

851. In *Ndola City Council v. Charles Mwansa,*[82] the Supreme Court held that an appeal does not act as a stay of execution and a party must apply for a stay of execution separately.

852. The Constitution of Zambia constitutes the Supreme Court of Zambia as a court. It has jurisdiction to hear and determine appeals in civil and criminal matters from the Court of Appeal. It also has jurisdiction as conferred on it by other laws.[83]

853. However, when appealing to the Supreme Court, a litigant is obliged to first obtain leave to appeal. In other words, they must obtain permission from the court to appeal to the Supreme Court. Section 13(3) of the Court of Appeal Act stipulates as follows:

> (3) The Court may grant leave to appeal where it considers that:
>
> (a) the appeal raises a point of law of public importance;

---

78. (1982) Z.R. 172 (S.C.).
79. Also confirmed in *Khalid Mohamed v. Attorney-General* (1982) Z.R. 49.
80. Appeal No. 42/2010.
81. SCZ No. 15 of 1999.
82. (1994) S.J.Z 78 (S.C.).
83. Article 125(2)(b) of the Constitution.

(b) it is desirable and in the public interest that an appeal by the person convicted should be determined by the Supreme Court;
(c) the appeal would have a reasonable prospect of success; or
(d) there is some other compelling reason for the appeal to be heard.

854. It should be noted that the factors above are disjunctive, meaning that only one of the conditions in the list suffices for the granting of leave to appeal. A litigant need only prove that one of the above factors to be eligible to get permission to appeal to the Supreme Court.

855. In the case of *Bidvest Food Zambia Limited and 4 Others v. CAA Import and Export Limited*,[84] the Supreme Court stated that there are three different facets of the qualifying criteria for leave to be granted must be satisfied, namely, a point of law; of public importance; and raised in the appeal. The Supreme Court emphasised the need for an appeal from the Court of Appeal to the Supreme Court to meet the requirements in section 13(3) for leave to appeal to be granted particularly where novel issues of public important or public interest or policy are involved.

856. The Supreme Court was emphatic that where an appeal from the Court of Appeal raises points of law of public importance that extends beyond purely ordinary questions, leave to appeal will be granted. However, not all novel issues will raise a point of law of public importance – only those which engaged wider public interest would be granted leave to appeal.

857. In the recent Supreme Court Ruling of *Musonda Mutale v. African Banking Corporation Limited*,[85] leave to appeal to the Supreme Court was denied because the case did not raise a novel issue or point of law of public importance.

858. On the hearing of an appeal in an employment matter, the Supreme Court may confirm, vary, amend or set aside the judgment appealed from or give such judgment as the case may require.[86] The Supreme Court is the final court of appeal unless the matter involves a dispute relating to the Constitution, in which case the Constitutional Court is the highest court.

859. If it appears to the Court that a new trial should be held, the Court has the power to set aside the judgment appealed against and order a new trial to be held. Whenever the Court gives instructions for the taking of further evidence, it is obliged to make such order as will secure an opportunity to the parties to the proceedings to examine every witness whose evidence is taken.[87]

---

84. Appeal No. 56/2017.
85. SCZ/8/05/2020.
86. Section 25(1).
87. Section 25.

860. Article 125(3) of the Constitution provides that the Supreme Court is bound by its decisions, except in the interests of justice and development of jurisprudence. Where the Supreme Court contradicts a previous Supreme Court decision, the lower courts are bound by the latest decision.

861. In *Davis Jokie Kasote v. The People,*[88] the Supreme Court, per Baron DCJ, held that a lower court cannot rely on a Supreme Court judgment that has been contradicted by a later judgment, even if that later judgment does not refer to an earlier decision.[89]

862. The Constitutional Court ranks equally with the Supreme Court. Any matter relating to the Constitution of Zambia shall be heard by the Constitutional Court. The Constitutional Court also has power to review any legislation or statutory instrument and set it aside if it contravenes to the Constitution.

863. The Constitutional Court has original and final jurisdiction to determine a matter relating to the interpretation of the Constitution. This means that in the employment law context, a party may commence an action directly with the Court to determine an issue touching on the interpretation of the constitution. The Industrial Relations Division is obliged to refer any questions relating to the Constitution to the Constitutional court according to section 128(2) of the Constitution which states that where a question relating to this Constitution arises in a court, the person presiding in that court shall refer the question to the Constitutional Court.

§2. Time Limits

864. A decision of the Tribunal shall be in writing and shall contain the following: the finding of the Tribunal on each issue of fact or law raised in the proceedings; and the reason for the Tribunal's findings.

865. The decision of the Competition and Consumer Protection Tribunal shall be made by the Tribunal within sixty days after hearing the appeal or application. According to the Court of Appeal in the cases of *Guardall Security Group Limited v. Reinford Kabwe*[90] and *ZEGA Limited v. The Zambia Revenue Authority,*[91] a decision of a court or Tribunal outside the mandatory period is null and void and without any legal effect.

866. A person aggrieved with a decision of the Competition and Consumer Protection Tribunal may appeal to the High Court within thirty days of the determination.

---

88. (1977) ZR 75 (S.C.).
89. *See also Zambia Consolidated Copper Mines Limited v. Patrick Mulemwa* SCZ Judgment No. 15 of 1995 which states that until such time as an earlier decision of the Supreme Court is upset by the Supreme Court itself, such decision remains binding on all other courts.
90. CAZ Appeal No. 44/2019.
91. CAZ Appeal No. 96/2018.

867. In a recent ruling of the High Court, the Court observed that a party that did not appeal against a decision of the Commission within thirty days lost the right to appeal. There is no set period within which an appeal from the Tribunal can be heard, except to mention that matters brought to the High Court by way of appeal are dealt with expeditiously.

§3. Scope of Judicial Review

868. Article 94 of the Constitution provides the extent of the powers of the High Court of Zambia to review administrative actions. The Court has unlimited and original jurisdiction to hear and determine any civil or criminal proceedings under any law. The position is, however, different in the UK where the courts have such jurisdiction as is prescribed in legislation enacted by Parliament.

869. Both Section 31 of the Supreme Court of the England and Order 53 of the Rules of the Supreme Court govern applications for judicial review. They identify the remedies available and the procedure to be followed to obtain public law remedies.

870. In Zambia, the Constitution has conferred upon the High Court original and unlimited jurisdiction to hear and determine any issue. There is no limit to the issues, which may be presented before the Court. The High Court can hear any civil or criminal matter. The Constitution does not, however, specify the remedies, which may be given by the Court. The array of remedies is, therefore, equally unlimited. The remedies given are dependent upon the nature of the case and what the party has prayed for.

871. The subject of the application for judicial review can be quashed on the ground of 'illegality', 'irrationality', and 'procedural impropriety' and the relief of mandamus granted.

872. A decision of the Competition and Consumer Protection Tribunal is flawed if it is illegal and hence reviewable by a court on this basis. A decision is illegal if: a) it contravenes or exceeds the terms of the power which authorises the making of the decision; or b) it pursues an objective other than that for which the power to make the decision was conferred.

873. The nature of 'illegality' is a primary ground for judicial review of administrative decisions. It is constituted by a public body consciously or unconsciously exceeding its express or implied statutory or de facto powers, or misconstruing the extent of its duties. Evidence of dishonest conduct, bad faith, or merely innocent misconstruction of matters of law, procedural irregularities, contravening mandatory provisions, or unreasonableness which thwarts the policy behind legislation have all been described as illegality in various cases, although they can also be brought within other categories of grounds for review; the precise classification of the alleged wrong is no longer important. Allegations of illegality are common in cases where the extent of statutory discretion is in issue. The court cannot determine the 'right' way to exercise a discretionary power; it can only indicate the parameters of the powers.

874. Lawful scope depends primarily on the construction of the Competition and Consumer Protection Act which outlines the powers concerned. Conduct can be expressly or impliedly unlawful, or substantively or procedurally unlawful. Statutes containing words such as 'shall' and 'may' invite a decision as to the nature of the authority given by the provision concerned. They may be imperative or permissive and disputes involving this issue raise questions of illegality. There may be a duty to act in a certain way whenever the promotion of the policy of the Competition and Consumer Protection Act so requires in the absence of a good reason for not acting. The courts may, despite the fact that the language of the Competition and Consumer Protection Act is couched in absolute terms, hold that an apparently unfettered discretion is limited in general legal obligations, imposed on the body concerned.

875. Other instance of illegality based on the interpretation of the Competition and Consumer Protection Act usually involve a mistake by the public body about the relevance of the considerations it has taken into account or failed to take into account or, alternatively actions which negate the assumed purpose of the legislation in question. It has been held by the House of Lords that parties may refer to Hansard in respect of statements of promoters of Bills so as to assist the court with regard to the policy behind the legislation.[92]

876. Improper Purpose: Officials may act with motives unrelated in a legal sense to the purpose of the statutory powers. In *Padfield v Minister of Agriculture Fisheries and Food,*[93] the minister refused to refer to a complaint to a statutory committee because he might be politically embarrassed by a favourable fining, despite the fact that he had a statutory role to play in the referral of complaints. This may not be clear to the official concerned until the court has given its opinion on the implied purpose behind the provision in question or the extent of the powers incidental to or consequential upon that which is expressly authorised. It is not unusual for the court to use the principles of constitutional law or administrative morality as principles for statutory interpretation governing the determination of the legality of the conduct.

877. Matters of Law: Sometimes the jurisdiction of public officials to embark upon or fulfil the decision-making part of their function will depend upon the construction of words of apparent ambiguity and their application to an individual or a situation. In such a situation it must be determined whether the construction in question is one which Parliament intended to be left to the decision-making body.

92. *Pepper v. Hart* [1993] 1 All ER 42, [1992] 3 WLR 1032.
93. [1968] AC997, [1968] 1 All ER 694.

878. Procedural Ultra Vires: Some statutes do not lay down procedure for the fulfilment of a statutory duty or exercise of the power, failure to comply with it may render the action taken ultra vires. Procedural obligations may be directory or mandatory or both in the sense that they may be mandatory but capable of substantial as opposed to absolute compliance. If the procedure is mandatory, the court will, subject to other discretionary principles, generally grant the relief. If it is directory only, the court will not need to consider the discretionary granting of the relief because the default will not have been intra vires.

879. A public body will be open to challenge where it has acted unfairly towards the applicant, by failing to observe basic rules of natural justice, or failing to act with procedural fairness. Even where the applicant has not been denied natural justice, there may be good challenge where the public body has failed to observe procedural rules expressly laid down by statute or delegated legislation.[94]

880. When considering statutory requirements, the courts are less concerned with the distinctions such as that between mandatory and directory requirements, and more with the desirability of achieving justice in a particular case. The court may not only require that the procedure prescribed by statute is followed, but may also imply additional procedural safeguards so as to ensure the attainment of fairness.

881. Failure to perform a duty to consult, or failure to satisfy legitimate expectation of consultation, are grounds for application. This is so especially where groups of citizens are aggrieved by the actions of public bodies.

882. A distinction must be drawn between a duty of fair consultation arising from statute and a duty to satisfy a legitimate expectation. The applicant should always look for the former. Failure to perform a statutory duty will amount to procedural impropriety which, subject to the court's discretion will entitle an applicant to judicial review. In the latter case, even if the decision maker fails in his duty, a later decision-making process may rectify the earlier unfairness.

883. Where Competition and Consumer Protection Act expressly defines those entitled to be consulted, such as section 64(2) of the Competition and Consumer Protection Act which provided the Commission shall consider any representations an enterprise wishes to make before making an application to enforce directions or undertakings, it is unlikely that others will claim the right. Where statute provides for a power to consult such bodies as appear representative, then the discretion as to who is to be consulted is reviewable on Wednesbury grounds.

884. Fair consultation means:

– consultation when the proposals are still at formative stage.

94. *Council of Civil Service Unions v. Minister for the Civil Service* [1985] AC 374, [1984] 3 All ER 945.

- adequate information to which to respond,
- adequate time in which to respond, and
- conscientious consideration by authority of the response to consultation.

885. A decision may be treated as invalid merely in relation to the party not consulted, and the court may in its discretion refuse to quash regulations made in the absence of mandatory consultations, where great inconvenience would result.

886. Natural Justice and Fairness: The rules of natural justice are the minimum standards of fairness imposed by the common law. The common law recognises two rules: *audi alteram partem* (hear the other side) and *nemo judex causa sua* (no one may be judge in their own cause). The applicant has the choice of relying on either fairness or natural justice.

887. In relation to legitimate expectations, Lord Denning was the first to distinguish legitimate expectation from the right or interest; an expectation of which it will be unfair to deprive the applicant without hearing what he had to say.[95] The words of Lord Diplock need to be taken into account first. He held that the decision in question must affect a person either:

(1) by altering rights or obligations of that person enforceable by or against him; or
(2) by depriving him of some benefit or advantage:
    (a) he had been permitted by the decision maker to enjoy and which he could legitimately expect to be permitted to do so unless there had been communicated to him some rational grounds for withdrawing it on which had been given an opportunity to comment; or
    (b) he had received assurance from the decision maker that the benefit or advantage would not be withdrawn without giving him first an opportunity of advancing some reasons for contending that they should not be drawn.

888. In recent cases the courts have insisted that there are five conditions which must be satisfied before an application bases on legitimate expectation can be satisfied:

(a) there must be a clear and unambiguous representation by the public body;
(b) the applicant must be within the class of persons entitled to rely on the representations;
(c) the applicant must have relied on it;
(d) this reliance must have been to his detriment;
(e) there must be no overriding public interest entitling the public body to change its policy to the detriment of the applicant.

---

95. *Schmidt v. Secretary of State for Home Affairs* [1969] 2 Ch 149, [1969] 1 All ER 904.

889. National security considerations will permit the government to fail to consult or to give a hearing where otherwise such failure would be challengeable. Principles of fairness may also, very exceptionally, be relaxed by reasons of emergency. It should also be borne in mind that the rules of natural justice are concerned with the propriety of the decision maker; an applicant cannot complain if he had no hearing through the fault of his legal advisors.

890. The individual must be told of the case he must meet. Even Rule 29 of the Competition and Consumer Protection (Tribunal) Rules provides that the Tribunal shall observe the principles of natural justice and shall hear all the evidence tendered and representations made by, or on behalf of, the parties or application.

891. Thus, parties must have a fair opportunity to react or contradict that case, and sufficient time to prepare an answer. The decision makers should not rely on points not argued before them, must disclose reports or other evidence upon which they propose to rely, and should not rely on their private investigations.

892. In some circumstances, all relevant evidence must be disclosed, as that which is protected by public policy; but the courts have also permitted public bodies to disclose the substance rather than the details of a case. The individual may, depending on the circumstances, be entitled to put his case orally or in writing; may have a right to examine witnesses, and may have a right to legal representation.

893. The second rule of natural justice is that the decision maker must have no material interest, whether by way of gain or detriment, in the outcome of proceedings unless such interest has been disclosed and no objection or objection waived.

894. Where the decision maker has a direct pecuniary interest, bias will be conclusively presumed. Where there is a non-pecuniary interest, the court has in part been concerned with upholding the principal that justice, must not only be done, but must be seen to be done.

895. Non-pecuniary interest may take the form of family connection; personal friendship, active interest in an organisation; previous involvement in the case; constant during an adjournment; or preconceived views.

896. Irrationality is a ground used in judicial review proceedings for challenging the quality of a decision, by reference to reasoning behind it.

897. Irrationality applies 'to a decision which is so outrageous in its defiance of logic or of the accepted moral standards that no sensible person who had applied his mind to the question to be decided could have arrived at it.'

898. The relevancy of matters considered by decision-making bodies must be taken out from the express provisions in the Constitution, The Competition and Consumer Protection Act, the regulations or the general common law, in cases of ambiguity. Where the law requires an official to be satisfied of something before taking action, the court will investigate the existence of the underlying facts and leave the evaluation of those factors to the decision maker, unless the evidence suggests that the weight given to the aspects of the evaluation was itself unreasonable.

899. It must be noted that the absence of reasons for a decision will not of itself support the contention of irrationality, since there is no general duty to give reasons in administrative law.[96] The mere existence of admissible reasons in favour of the respondent's decision is not enough to stop a finding of irrationality, because it will still consider their rationality nonetheless.

900. The court will intervene where the facts taken as a whole could not logically warrant the conclusion of the decision maker, for instance that the evidence is overwhelmingly in favour of the opposite conclusion.

901. The court will normally examine both the rationality of the findings of fact on which the impugned decision is based, and that of the decision maker's evaluation of those facts, in concluding as he did. The court will grant the relief where there is some evidence of pointing to the finding, that no reasonable tribunal could have regarded it as sufficient to warrant such a finding. Giving undue weight[97] even to a legitimate consideration might turn it into an irrelevance.[98]

902. Sometimes the court will be persuaded that there was no evidence at all to support a finding of fact made by a decision maker.[99] It must be noted that in relation to 'no evidence' cases quashing a decision when no weight has been given to a consideration necessary forming part of the statutory purpose, is simply quashing for illegality. Alternatively, it can be argued that if a decision is made and there was simply no evidence to support it, then it has been made irrational.

903. This sort of intervention by the judiciary is not merely correcting mistakes of fact made by the decision makers. In theory the court will be countenance acting as an appellate court. The court in such a situation is merely ensuring that decisions are made for which there is rational basis, without interfering with the decision makers function of resolving disputed matters of fact within his jurisdiction.

96. It was however, observed by *Lord Donaldson in R v. Lancshire County Counci*l, ex p. Hudleston [1986] 2 All ER 941 that generally speaking public bodies should at least be ready to assist the court, with a full explanation of why they have acted or decided in a particular way.
97. See West Glamoragn County Council v Rafferty [1987] 1 All ER 1005, [1987] 1 WLR 457.
98. *Police Complaints Board, ex p. Madden* [1983] 2 All ER 353, [1983] 1 WLR 447, *R v. South Oxfordshire DC v. Secretary of State for Environment* [1981] 1 All ER 954, [1981] 1 WLR 1092.
99. *Sagnata Investments Limited v Norwich Corporation* [1971] 2QB 614, [1971] 2 All ER 1441.

Selected Bibliography

Legislation

Employment Code Act No. 3 of 2019
English Extent of Application Act, Chapter 4 of the Laws of Zambia
Companies Act No. 10 of 2017
Competition and Consumer Protection Act No. 24 of 2010
Competition and Consumer Protection (General) Regulations, Statutory Instrument No. 97 of 2011
Competition and Consumer Protection (Tribunal) Regulations, Statutory Instrument No. 37 of 2012

Zambian Cases

Anthony Khetani Phiri v. Workers Compensation Control Board SCZ Judgment No. 2 of 2003.
Ethiopian Airlines Limited v. Sunbird Safaris Limited and 2 Others SCZ Judgment No. 26 of 2007
Insurance Association of Zambia and Others v. The Competition and Consumer Protection Commission 2018/CCPTC/002/COM
MRI Seed Zambia and Others v. Amiran Zambia Limited Appeal No. 2017/CCPT/001/CON.
National Milling Company Limited v. Grace Simataa and Others (2000) Z.R. 91 (S.C.).
Samuel Liato & Milandu Sichikolo v. National Pension Scheme Authority Comp/IRCLK/457/2017.
Wynter M Kabimba v. The Attorney General and Lusaka City Council SCZ Judgment No. 13 of 1996.

Selected Bibliography

Index

The numbers here refer to paragraph numbers.

Index

www.ingramcontent.com/pod-product-compliance
Lightning Source LLC
Chambersburg PA
CBHW071342230926
51846CB00002B/417
9789403542157